A Short History of Ontario

Dr. Ed Whitcomb

From Sea to Sea Enterprises

Ottawa

Library and Archives Canada Cataloguing in Publication

Whitcomb, Dr. Edward A.
A Short History of Ontario / Ed Whitcomb.

Includes bibliographical references and index.
ISBN 978-0-9694667-6-5

1. Ontario – History. I. Title.

FC3061.W438 2007 971.3
C2007-905466-8

© From Sea To Sea Enterprises, 2007
2130 Dutton Crescent, Ottawa,
Ontario, Canada, K1J 6K4

Printed in Canada by Dollco Printing, Ottawa

TABLE OF CONTENTS

This Book is Dedicated to the
people of Ontario

Preface

This is the fifth in a series of history books on Canada's ten provinces. The idea for this series first arose in 1969 when I moved to Nova Scotia. Being new to the province and knowing very little about it, I went looking for a short history book which would provide an outline of the development of my newly-adopted home. There was no such book. In fact, there were hardly any short histories of Canada's provinces. In 1975 I decided to write the sort of book I had been looking for, and started with my native province of Manitoba. Over 8,000 copies of that Short History of Manitoba have been sold, which suggests that I was not alone in wanting good, short provincial histories. The project to write histories of all the provinces was delayed by family and career, but the Centennials of Alberta and Saskatchewan put the series back on track, and the short histories of those provinces were published in 2005.

This Short History of Ontario is designed to provide the average reader with a quick but accurate survey of the broad outline of Ontario's development. The emphasis in this book is on the political developments that shaped the province as it is today, subjects such as the natives, immigration and settlement, economic activities like the fur trade, farming and mining, and the attainment of provincial status.It explains the reasons for the boom that preceded the First World War and the depression that followed, including such issues as prohibition and women's suffrage. The Depression, World War II, the Big Blue Machine, and more modern developments complete the account.

Every historian has a point of view that determines which of the thousands of issues he or she will discuss, which of the millions of facts he or she will relate, and what things he or she will emphasize or ignore. This is essentially a political history, with some reference to economic and social developments, and it clearly emphasizes provincial rather than national or local developments. It seeks to explain Ontario's side in disputes between the province and the federal government. It is not "popular history", and does not include pictures because there are several excellent picture books of Ontario. While the achievements of Ontarians are documented, some criticisms are made of the heroes, politicians and groups who have shaped the province. In short, it is but one perspective on a very fascinating and complex society.My greatest hope is that this small book will encourage others to read more and to write more on the dozens of issues and perspectives necessary to obtain a full understanding of any society's development.

This account ends with the mid-1980s.Several readers thought it should cover more recent developments, but there is a point where history merges into political science or journalism. While we know the broad outline of recent events, we do not have access to Cabinet decisions, correspondence or the memoirs of most participants.Many issues are still current, some still the subject of sharp debate, and many views on them are more subjective than objective. Much research has to be done and many books and articles written before the recent past falls into a proper historical perspective. Perhaps a revised edition in 2025 will bring the story up to 2007!

Many people helped with the preparation of this book. A number of professors, editors, analysts and experts read the full text and made many valuable corrections and suggestions. They include Dr. R. Matthew Bray, Dr. Penny Bryden, Dr. Gerald Friesen, John Hannigan, Alex Inglis, Robert Poetschke, Dr. Ron Stagg, and Dr. Randall White. I alone am responsible for the weaknesses that remain in the book.The cover designs and maps were done by Linda Turenne, and the colours are those of the official Ontario flag. Chomchon Tummanon did the formatting and page layouts. John Colyer of Dollco Printers helped with the technical details.Most helpful of all were my wife, Kai, and daughters Denise and Diana whose support and patience made the book possible.

Ottawa, December, 2007.

Chapter One
Natives, Settlement and the Founding of Canada, to 1812

The present-day province of Ontario is enormous, covering over one million square kilometers. It is Canada's second largest province, measuring 1,600 kilometers from east to west and 1,600 from north to south. It is a land of enormous variety. Ontario can be divided into five distinct geographical regions, but the lines between them are blurred as one melds into the next. In the southwest corner, between Lakes Erie and Huron, lies an area of flat, extremely rich agricultural land, one of the prime bases of Ontario's wealth. When the Europeans first arrived it was covered by dense hardwood forests. Northeast of that is a belt about 100 kilometers wide running from Kingston to Georgian Bay, featuring rolling hills, and pockets of agricultural land mixed with hardwood forest.

Farther north is another band around 200 kilometers wide running from the Ottawa River to the eastern shore of Lake Huron. This is an area of mixed forest, of deciduous trees like beech, maple, and poplar, and of coniferous trees like white and red pine and spruce. North of that, running from Quebec to Manitoba, is the largest geographic area. Here the Precambrian Shield of ancient rock often comes to the surface. That feature and the cool climate limit vegetation to coniferous or softwood trees and scrub brush in the areas not covered by rock, lake and muskeg. These forests and some of the richest mineral deposits in the world constitute two more bases of Ontario's great wealth. Farther north, around Hudson Bay and James Bay are the lowlands, where poor drainage and cold climate produce an inhospitable landscape of muskeg and swamp.

Southern Ontario is blessed with a wealth of rivers and lakes. Indeed, geography gave Ontario its name for the native word means "rocks standing by water". The Great Lakes are one of the best inland waterways in the world, with Lakes Ontario, Erie, Huron and Superior forming most of the southern border of the province. Explorers and fur traders traveled relatively easily from Montreal to Lake Huron using the Ottawa River, the Mattawa River, Lake Nipissing, and the French River. Another series of lakes and canals connect Lake Ontario and Georgian Bay via the Trent River. Numerous rivers like the Thames, Grand and Rideau carried settlement and trade inland. In the south, this geography was near-perfect for settlement – hospitable climate, good soil, easy access to rivers and lakes, wood for lumber and fuel, and rivers and streams to harness for flour and saw mills. In Northern Ontario, in contrast, rivers run southwards into Lake Superior or northwards towards Hudson Bay and James Bay, and are not easily connected.

Present-day Ontario was discovered, explored and settled by native peoples who came from Asia over12, 000 years ago. Each wave of migration pushed the earlier inhabitants farther south and east, and they probably entered Ontario around 11,000 years ago. The Natives who migrated into this region belonged to two broad language groups, and probably numbered between 50,000 and 100,000 in the early seventeenth century when Europeans first arrived. In the north were the Algonkian speakers belonging to six main tribes, the Cree, Algonkin, Nipissing, Mississauga, Ottawa and Ojibwa or Chippewa. These tribes lived primarily by hunting, fishing and gathering nuts and berries, and traveled widely in their brilliant invention, the birch bark canoe. In the south were the Iroquoian speakers, the Huron, Erie, Petun, and Neutral.

Native society was communal rather than individualistic as in white society, a distinction that has survived despite centuries of effort by whites to break it down. Natives had no concept of owning land. Their gods had provided land, water and resources for all the people. Those who could hunt and fish did so, acquired what was needed, and shared with others. Tribes fought wars over the right to fish or hunt in certain areas, not over the ownership of those areas. Religion acknowledged creation, and emphasized the concept of harmony between man and nature and within each tribe. Bands had religious leaders known as shamans who were also medicine men, administering to the ill with a combination of herbal remedies and spirit worship. Concepts of acceptable and unacceptable behaviour were highly developed, and seem to have been followed with little need for discipline. Concepts of ownership were fairly loose – if something was there, it could be used, a practice Europeans tended to see as theft.

France laid claim to southern Ontario in 1534 when Jacques Cartier landed in Quebec and claimed the region drained by the St. Lawrence River for the King of France. The earliest contact between the natives and Europeans probably occurred when the French fur trader Étienne Brûlé paddled up the Ottawa River in 1610. Three years later Samuel de Champlain began exploring the Ottawa River and eventually Georgian Bay. At the same time the English explorer, Henry Hudson, sailed into the bay that bears his name, claiming for England all the land drained by rivers flowing northwards, including about one half of modern Ontario.

The basis of contact between the natives and Europeans soon became the fur trade. The lakes and swamps of Ontario were the habitat of the beaver, and its fur was in high demand in Europe. The Europeans had numerous trade items of great value to the natives – rifles, steel knives, copper pots, various implements, and wool blankets. The Hurons south of Georgian Bay quickly established themselves as middlemen between the French in Montreal and the tribes further inland. For several generations a Huron civilization had thrived on corn and furs. Near Midland French missionaries helped construct a mission known as Ste. Marie among the Hurons. English merchants in New York competed with the French from the south, and after 1670 the Hudson's Bay Company controlled the trade in northern Ontario. The natives cleverly exploited this choice of markets defying all attempts by the Europeans to monopolize the trade.

South of the Great Lakes the Five Nations of the Iroquois Confederacy became the middlemen in the fur trade between the Dutch and later the English colony in New York and the tribes farther inland. That made them rivals of the Hurons. Natives had always fought over fishing and hunting lands, but the new importance of controlling the fur trade plus the introduction of rifles dramatically increased the viciousness of warfare. The Huron were devastated by European diseases like smallpox for which they had no immunity - disease destroyed half the Huron nation in 1638. In this weakened state, Huron villages were rapidly destroyed by the Iroquois.

During this period the French established a number of posts, as centres for the fur trade and to protect their colony from attack by the English to the south. They included Fort Frontenac (Kingston), Fort Niagara, Fort Detroit, and Fort Michilimackinac near Sault Ste Marie. From the St. Lawrence-Great Lakes system the French explored the rivers and lakes of Ontario, and ventured on to the Rockies and the Gulf of Mexico. Small settlements grew up around these forts, mainly to provide vegetables for the garrisons. One of these, at Windsor across the river from Fort Detroit, is probably the oldest European settlement in Ontario.

In 1756 France and England began a decisive war for global dominance including the control of North America. The tide of war gradually turned against the French, with the English capturing Fort Frontenac in 1758, Fort Niagara and Quebec City in 1759, and Montreal and Detroit in 1760. By the Treaty of Paris of 1763 New France and the inhabitants who called themselves Canadiens passed to English control, and southern Ontario became part of the new British colony of Quebec.

British rule brought few changes to the part of Quebec that lay west of the Ottawa River. The fur trade passed from French to British hands, the new masters carrying on the systems created by the French, and employing the same French traders to collect furs in Ontario. Fort William (Thunder Bay) was developed as the half-way point between the supply base of Montreal and a fur trade empire that eventually extended to British Columbia. In the forts, British troops replaced French ones, but the French settlers around the forts continued growing their crops and feeding the garrisons. Britain did not want trouble with the natives in Ontario such as Chief Pontiac of the Ottawa Nation, nor with the natives south of the Great Lakes. It also saw the natives as potential allies should relations deteriorate further with the American colonists. Accordingly, it passed the Royal Proclamation of 1763 forbidding settlement south of the Great Lakes.

The American colonists wanted to expand westward, and British opposition to that expansion became one of their main grievances. Another grievance was the Quebec Act, passed in 1774 to provide a governmental structure for the new colony. The British decided that the best way to govern their 60-70,000 French Canadian colonists was to leave them alone, and the Quebec Act guaranteed their Roman Catholic religion, French language, civil law, and system of land ownership. Unlike the colonies to the south, Quebec was clearly run by a Governor, with no elected assembly to modify or challenge his decisions. The Quebec Act also confirmed that the borders of Quebec would be those of New France, leaving the lands south of the Great Lakes unavailable for westward expansion by the American colonists.

The Quebec Act helped propel the thirteen American colonies into a war of independence. Ontario was virtually untouched by the fighting, but it was a base for British officers to organize native attacks on the western American frontier. The Americans won the war, which produced profound effects on Ontario. One was that the border between Quebec and the United States was fixed at midway in the St. Lawrence River and Lakes Ontario, Erie, Huron and Superior, and overland to Lake of the Woods. Secondly, around 10,000 people left the United States to settle along the north shore of the St. Lawrence and in the Niagara Peninsula. Most of them were Loyalists or supporters of Britain, and they were conservative in their views. They were mainly English and Anglican, but included natives, Scottish Catholics, Germans, French Protestants, Black Africans and some British soldiers, and they were more American than British in everything but loyalty.

The land they occupied was purchased from the natives who may not have understood the legal implications of "selling". It was surveyed into districts and eventually into counties and townships, names that still identify the roads and boundaries of today's countryside. Officers in the British Army received 1,000 acres of land; lesser ranks 200 acres. They were given transportation, implements, seeds, and financial support, the latter lasting for many years in some cases.

Most of these settlers were farmers, and had lived for generations in North America, in a climate and environment similar to southern Ontario. Within months they had felled trees, built temporary shacks to keep out the rain and snow, planted crops between the tree stumps, begun hacking trails through the dense forest, and started the backbreaking labour of removing huge tree stumps. The best way to get rid of the trees was to fell them and burn them, and the resulting ash or potash became the first cash crop. With the arrival of settlers, small towns began to develop with tradesmen, merchants, blacksmiths, inns, lawyers, and doctors – Cornwall, Prescott, Brockville and Gananoque along the St. Lawrence. At the same time, the garrison towns of Kingston and Niagara developed into service centres.

Another group of settlers was the Five Nations or Iroquois, mostly Mohawks, who had fought on the King's side. A large group under Chief Joseph Brant was given a block of land along the Grand River by the future town of Brantford. Others under Chief Desoronto settled in the Bay of Quinte and east of Cornwall, their land grants being interspersed with those of the Loyalists. They often sold their land to white settlers, though it was not quite clear whether they had sold the land or leased it. Natives remained a major part of the population until the large British migration of the early nineteenth century.

The Quebec Act of 1774 had been designed to recognize the religious, legal, and social values of the Canadiens in New France and to provide strong, authoritarian government. But the English-speaking Protestant Loyalists and the non-Loyalist American settlers who migrated into the St. Lawrence-Great Lakes region had different attitudes towards life, work, education, commerce, land ownership, and the role of government and religion. They brought the American belief that in making his decisions, the governor should listen to the views of the people, as expressed through elected Legislative Assemblies as was the case in the thirteen American colonies. These ideas could not be accommodated within the framework of the Quebec Act, and the British Parliament replaced it with the Constitutional or Canada Act of 1791.

Although the name Canada had appeared on maps for many years, this Act established Canada as a legal, political and constitutional entity. It was divided into the provinces of Upper Canada (present-day Ontario) and Lower Canada (Quebec). Canada was a native name that the French explorer Jacques Cartier first heard in 1534, and Upper refers to the higher elevation of the St. Lawrence. The border of Upper Canada began just west of Montreal, and then ran along the Ottawa River to the lands of the Hudson's Bay Company.

Power in the new colony of Upper Canada still rested with a Governor, resident in Quebec City but was delegated to a Lieutenant Governor. The latter was authorized to appoint an Executive Council of assistants to head government departments, men who owned at least 6,000 acres of land. Replicating the British House of Lords would be an Advisory Council, appointed by the Governor from the leading members of the Loyalist and British elite. They were appointed for life, part of the structure designed to create some sort of hereditary aristocracy in the nascent colony.

The demand for a Legislative Assembly was met, with elections every four years. The Assembly's powers were limited, however, because the British Government believed that the excessive power of the American assemblies had been a major factor in the movement for independence. The Assemblies could vote or withhold taxes, but the Governor was given sufficient sources of revenues to render him almost independent of the Assembly. The qualification for voting was possession of a certain amount of property, but almost every adult male in Upper Canada actually owned land. Other measures reflected the British character of the new colony. The Quebec system of land measurement and ownership was abolished, English common law was adopted in Upper Canada, and English alone would be the language of the new government.

One-seventh of the colony was set aside as Crown Reserves for future sale as a source of revenue. Another one-seventh was set aside as the Clergy Reserves. At this time, churches played an enormous role in society, providing education, health, and welfare in addition to the spiritual needs of a very religious and devout population. The remaining land was used to reward or compensate Loyalists, to reward loyalty or service to the new regime, to help create a new, pro-British aristocracy, or to attract settlers.

The idea of giving the church one-seventh of the land was not controversial, but the government decided to reserve all of that land for the Anglican Church of England. That decision reflected the belief that an essentially English political and social system could and should be imposed on the new colony, and part of that system was the Anglican Church. Only a minority of the population was Anglican, and the Clergy Reserves soon created serious problems without achieving their social goals.

These land policies created problems from the beginning of the colony and seriously inhibited its development for decades. In order to realize the greatest income from their land grants, government, clergy, many grantees and some farmers kept their land off the market waiting for property prices to rise. Poorer Loyalists and ordinary settlers acquired land and cleared it. Their land was then interspersed with undeveloped land retained for speculation, and the settlers found themselves paying for roads that ran past idle land that they could not afford to buy.

With the political, legal and constitutional framework approved, the British turned to the task of establishing a government. Colonel John Graves Simcoe was appointed Lieutenant Governor of Upper Canada. Simcoe was a tough, decisive and energetic British officer who had fought in the American War of Independence. He saw the American victory as a mistake or an accident, an unfortunate outcome that gave the rabble majority supremacy over the educated elite.

Simcoe set out to create the type of society that he thought should have prevailed south of the border. It would be British, royalist, ordered, disciplined, deferential, proper, decent, Anglican, and above all, law-abiding. Laws would be passed to ensure that all of these characteristics flourished in the new society. Those laws would be enforced by the new judicial system, staffed by Loyalists and housed in the magnificent court houses that were built in every county capital. The province was divided into 19 counties, the counties surveyed into townships of nine by 12 miles each. Large grants of land were given to Loyalists and to immigrants from England who could be counted on to become ruling members of the new aristocracy that would properly govern the colony.

The attempt to create an English aristocracy was a dismal failure. With free land readily available in the United States, few farmers were willing to work for a landlord. Simcoe therefore offered free land to American settlers knowing that they did not believe in the type of society he was attempting to create. They came in the thousands, because for American farmers, owning and developing their own farm was far more important than theoretical distinctions between monarchy and republic. In the first two decades after 1791 the population of Upper Canada exploded from 20,000 to 90.000, and that growth was overwhelmingly American. The would-be aristocrats, however, clung for decades to the dream of running the province, fighting a hopeless, rear-guard battle that seriously retarded the colony's advancement.

Immigration significantly changed the political and social composition of the province. "Real" Loyalists, ones who had fought for Britain became an increasingly small minority of the population. "Late Loyalists", ones who were not refugees and whose claims to free Loyalist land might be dubious, also became a diminishing portion of the population. New American settlers gradually became a majority. Methodists soon outnumbered Anglicans, making the Clergy Reserves a serious political issue.

Simcoe was also busy with other top priorities such as establishing government. The first Assembly met at Newark, present-day Niagara-on-the-Lake, on September 17, 1792. It consisted of an appointed Legislative Council and a Legislative Assembly of 16. That site was within a few miles of the American border, so the capital was moved the following year to York on the north shore of Lake Ontario. York had been a French trading post, was relatively safe from American attack, lay at the base of a land route from Lake Ontario to Lake Huron, and centered a large area of excellent agricultural land. It would adopt the native name Toronto in 1834, and eventually become the permanent capital of Ontario.

Another of Simcoe's top priorities was defence against the unfulfilled territorial dreams of the United States. He worked to strengthen the fortifications at Kingston, Niagara and York. He saw roads as crucial to both settlement and defence, and laid the basis for the main arteries of today's Ontario. They included Yonge Street, running north from York to Georgian Bay, Danforth (later Kingston) Road running east towards Montreal, and Dundas Street running west to Hamilton and London. He was right to concentrate on defence, for the Americans had never accepted the territorial provisions of the treaty of 1783. As American settlers flooded west over the Allegheny Mountains, and as tens of thousands of them settled in Upper Canada, it seemed natural to Americans that Upper Canada would soon be part of the USA.

Chapter Two
War, Development and Rebellion, 1812 – 1839

By 1812 the United States and Britain were drifting towards war. One American grievance was that British ships stopped American ones on the high seas and took escaped British sailors and some American ones for service in the Royal Navy. The Senators from the affected states, however, voted against war. More important grievances stemmed from the western frontier, where American expansion was hindered by British-supported natives. Conquering Upper Canada would solve that problem as well as providing another rich area for settlement, and it is those issues that led the United States to declare war on Britain on June 18, 1812. For Canada, the issue was whether it would be conquered and absorbed into the United States.

The British had been preparing for the war since the last one ended in 1783. All their policies had a military flavour – building roads, locating settlements near the border, creating county militias, settling war veterans, and creating a disciplined social and political order under a British and Loyalist elite. When war began in Ontario, the British had some important advantages. British ships dominated the Lakes, and though limited to just one regiment, British soldiers were disciplined and effective professionals.

Britain started the war with the best leader, Major General Sir Isaac Brock. Brock was smart, confident, courageous, decisive, and a brilliant tactician and strategist. Opposed to him were a number of American generals whose incompetence bordered on cowardice. The Americans army greatly outnumbered the British, but the quality of its soldiers was low. In addition, decades of assiduous attention to good relations with the natives paid off – under the brilliant Chief Tecumseh they put terror in the hearts of American troops and settlers.

As the war began, the great unknown was the loyalty of the American 60,000 settlers in Upper Canada. They cared about their farms and families, not about flags, politics, or international rivalries. They had little reason to be loyal to the governments in York or distant London, especially as they had been treated as second-class citizens. At best they might just sit out the war; at minimum they might help the Americans; at worst, they might join them.

The American strategy was dictated by geography: they would attack Canada up the Richelieu River to Montreal, at Niagara, and at the west end of Lake Erie opposite Detroit – Kingston was far too powerful to tackle. Brock sensed that the best defence would be a good offense. On August 15, 1812, he crossed the Detroit River, laid siege to the Americans in Detroit, who greatly outnumbered him, demanded and got their surrender. That was the first decisive victory of the war, though the Americans regained Detroit in 1813. Earlier the local British commander had seized Michilimackinac near Sault Ste Marie, giving Britain control of the upper lakes throughout the war.

Brock then moved east to Niagara to face the second thrust of the American strategy. Shortly after he arrived, the Americans who outnumbered the British four to one had captured Queenston Heights. Brock immediately launched a counter-attack. He was killed, but his second-in-command, General Roger Sheaffe, defeated the Americans, who lost 1,300 dead and 1,000 captured compared to British losses of 100. The third thrust – towards Montreal – also failed, and 1812 ended with British North America in British hands. Equally important, the American settlers in Upper Canada demonstrated little enthusiasm for helping the United States in its war of conquest.

The following year saw military stalemate. For the United States, however, that meant another year of failure. The fighting turned nasty, with considerable looting and property damage and both sides hanging civilians as traitors. American guerrilla attacks on civilians along the shore of Lake Erie proved counter-productive as previously neutral farmers turned to the British Army for protection. In April the Americans seized the capital of York. General Sheaffe blew up the powder magazine, killing and wounding 200 Americans. After burning the legislative buildings and indulging in some random looting and arson, the Americans abandoned York. A month later they took Fort George near Niagara-on-the-Lake. An American thrust into the Niagara Peninsula was defeated at Stoney Creek near Hamilton. In June an attempted surprise attack failed when Laura Secord overheard talk of it and warned the British. Natives defeated that American force at Beaver Dam.

To the west, the Americans gained control of Lake Erie. Finally under the able leadership of General William Henry Harrison, an American army moved up the Thames River and crushed General Proctor's force and its native allies at Moraviantown. The great Indian Chief Tecumseh was killed. The Americans failed to exploit their advantage, however, and retreated again to Detroit. The year ended with the Americans burning Niagara-on-the-Lake before retreating across the river. In retaliation the British crossed over and burnt Buffalo.

The third and last year of warfare was also one of stalemate. The Americans finally took Fort Erie, but were then defeated at Lundy's Lane in July. They then retreated once more across the river. By late 1814 both Britain and the United States were exhausted. The Treaty of Ghent reaffirmed the status quo in Upper Canada which makes it one of the most crucial treaties in Canadian history. Upper and Lower Canada remained British. The United States continued to expand, but the direction would be westwards, not northwards. Britain and Canada had won the War of 1812.

The British-Loyalist elite emerged from the war more determined than ever to maintain British institutions and to prevent the spread of republicanism, democracy and other American heresies. One of their first measures restricted American immigration. Attempts were made to deny American settlers the right to own property and vote. These policies helped keep Upper Canada British in institutions and sentiment, but they cut off the best supply of experienced settlers and doomed the province to economic stagnation for decades while states south of the Great Lakes surged ahead economically.

Fortunately, conditions in the British Isles soon favoured immigration, and tens of thousands set out for Canada. They were assisted by organizations like John Galt's Canada Company, which bought 2.5 million acres from the government, brought out settlers, and sold the land to them. Peter Robinson brought thousands of Irish to the area that took his name, Peterborough, and John Talbot helped settle a huge tract of land near Lake Erie. The largest group was from northern Ireland or Ulster, Presbyterians of Scottish descent. They were fiercely pro-British and bigoted in their anti-Catholic hatreds, a sentiment cultivated by their secretive Orange Lodge. They settled throughout the province, and had a profound impact on nineteenth-century Ontario.

The second largest group was probably Irish Catholic, socially similar to the Irish Protestants, equally devoted to their religion, but decidedly anti-British. Some settled in cities where their poverty created slum conditions, and they provided the backbone to construction, industry and forestry. Both groups were ethnically Celtic rather than Anglo-Saxon and some spoke Gaelic. Though Celtic Scots were less numerous, they exercised a disproportionate influence on politics and commerce. Another group that melded in more easily with the existing population came from England – wealthier than the Irish, mainly Anglican, and often including tradesmen and merchants. They settled all over the province, and formed much of the merchant and professional class.

Added to the mix was a smaller group of Highland Catholic Scots who settled near Cornwall and west of Toronto. In the east, French Canadians were settling the Ottawa River valley. By 1840 almost all of southwest Ontario had been cleared, and settlers had begun moving into the Canadian Shield. This immigration pushed the population from 90,000 in 1812 to around 230,000 in 1831 and close to 500,000 by 1842. It also changed profoundly the national balance, with those of British parentage eventually outnumbering the American element. Often thought of as "English" because of language, the majority was ethnically Celtic. In terms of religion, Anglicans were now the largest faction, followed by Methodists, Catholics and Presbyterians.

Immigrants and the pioneers' children pushed the frontier 10 to 20 miles back from the shores of Lakes Ontario and Erie and the rivers that flowed into them. Along the shore tree stumps were finally removed, the land leveled, and log houses replaced shacks, with the occasional wood-frame or brick house appearing. The rich soil of the southwest was ideally suited for wheat, and the British government favoured its importation – wheat would become the foundation of Ontario's wealth in the nineteenth century. Other crops prospered, and the fringe of settlement continued to produce lumber for domestic and foreign consumption. The introduction of the steam engine meant factories could be built anywhere, and slashed the costs and time for transportation within the colony and to Europe or the United States.

Kingston and Toronto grew into small cities of over 10,000, and dozens of towns with a few hundred people emerged. Each one had some merchants, a blacksmith, a cabinet maker, a miller, a bank, an inn, and several Protestant churches. Roads made of logs or crushed rock gradually replaced crooked mud trails. Stagecoaches appeared, with the boredom and discomfort of the journey relieved by roadside inns every five miles or so. They also did a roaring business with the local male population, liquor vying with religion to ease the hardships and tragedies of frontier life.

The overall economy became more diversified. In the Ottawa Valley giant trees were felled and squared. The square timber was floated down to Montreal, and exported to England. On the return voyage the ships were crammed with immigrants. Canal building was crucial to link the Lakes to Montreal, the Welland being completed in 1829. The Rideau Canal was completed in 1832 and the canals on the Ottawa in 1834, though all of these were originally designed more for military than economic reasons. Blacksmith shops began to manufacture agricultural machinery, and other industries made furniture, carriages, wagons, harnesses, casks, nails tools, china, clothing and linen goods. Food processing developed to supply cheese, butter, meat, beer and whiskey, with very different standards of measure, quality and safety. Many of these things, however, were made at home by processes that were crude, cheap, and terribly inefficient.

Some members of the Legislative and Executive Councils came to be known as the Family Compact. The name came from the fact that a small elite monopolized the key jobs, inter-married, and appointed relatives to government positions including the justices of the peace who provided local administration. Their supporters were known as Tories. Typical of them was John Strachan, first Anglican Bishop of Toronto, member of the Executive Council, and fierce defender of the privileges of the Anglican Church. With ties to the Montreal business elite, they preferred investment in canals to promote commerce rather than roads to help farmers get to town. The Compact allotted all the proceeds of the sale of Clergy Reserves to the Anglican Church, but was gradually forced to grant a share to the Presbyterian Church of Scotland and later to the Methodists.

High tariffs on imports raised the prices of consumer goods, but too much of the money went for the excessive salaries the Compact paid themselves and their appointees and too little for roads, schools or hospitals. The sale of the land grants they gave themselves further widened the gap between them and the populace. The fact that they ruled in their own interest was evident in banking policy – nine of 15 directors of the Bank of Upper Canada were members of the Legislative Council, and it rejected petitions to establish other banks. Secondary and post-secondary education was designed to give their children proper British and Anglican values and the skills necessary to follow their father's careers.

The first serious challenge to the Compact's authority came when a Scottish immigrant, Robert Gourlay, made a survey of the situation in the colony. It revealed sharp dissatisfaction with land policy, and he organized a convention to discuss it. He was banished for sedition, a law the Legislative Assembly tried repeatedly to abolish because of such abuse. The interests of the Family Compact and those of the majority as reflected in the Legislative Assembly drifted further apart, and the Assembly started to challenge the power of the Executive Council. In the 1824 elections, Reformers won a majority for the first time, and forced the government to abandon the attempts to deny rights to American-born settlers. Reformers solidly won the 1828 election, and Governor Peregrine Maitland decided to intervene directly to support the Family Compact. He helped the Tories win the election of 1830, but the Reformers were back in a majority after the 1834 vote.

In the 1820s and 30s the system of government envisaged in the Canada Act was clearly breaking down. After the War of 1812 the Assembly became increasingly frustrated as the legitimate needs of the populace were ignored and the Executive used its power for the advantage of the elite. A demand developed, led by William and Robert Baldwin, for Responsible Government. In that system of government, the Executive Council or Cabinet governs according to the wishes of the Assembly and remains in power only as long as it has the confidence of the Assembly.

The most damaging critic of the Compact was the sharp-tongued and irreverent William Lyon Mackenzie, owner of the Colonial Advocate. His newspaper attacks were so devastating that a group of his victims threw his printing press into Lake Ontario. He was repeatedly elected to the Assembly, and repeatedly expelled from it. The British responded to the situation by sending a new Governor, Sir Francis Bond Head. He appointed Robert Baldwin to the Executive Council, but then refused to accept his advice, prompting the entire Council to resign. In the ensuing election of 1836, Head campaigned vigorously for the Tory candidates, and generously dispensed patronage and appeals to loyalty to win the election.

The outbreak of rebellion in Lower Canada, the alleged rigging of the 1836 election and economic recession pushed Mackenzie and others towards violence. In 1837 he rallied a group of malcontents to armed rebellion, a pale reflection of the far more serious rebellion in Lower Canada. The main group assembled north of York on December 4, and marched down to Montgomery's tavern. In the mean time, the militia organized to meet them. Three days later, a brief skirmish sent the rebels fleeing. Mackenzie and many followers escaped to the United States. A couple of rebels were caught and executed and a lot more were imprisoned or banished to Australia.

For the Tories, however, it was a short-lived victory. The Government in London was well aware that both Upper and Lower Canada were badly governed and that the system itself was broken. The colony was costing Britain money because slow economic development, poor governance and strained relations with the Legislative Assembly were reducing tax collection. The ongoing political crisis was an invitation for American interference, and some Americans did, in fact, help Mackenzie. Britain had to fix government in Upper and Lower Canada so it sent a new Governor, Lord Durham, to study the situation and recommend solutions.

Chapter Three
From Failed Union to Successful Federation, 1839 – 1867

Lord Durham made three major recommendations. Britain accepted the idea of uniting Upper and Lower Canada to further the economic development of the whole St. Lawrence-Great Lakes region. It also accepted the recommendation to swamp the French Canadian population of Lower Canada politically and then force their assimilation into English Canada. It postponed, however, the recommendation which called for the implementation of Responsible Government. The decisions to postpone responsible government and assimilate the French Canadians set the stage for a political stalemate that lasted for over two decades. When it was over, Canada had the two institutions that have formed the basis of its political life ever since – democratic government, in which the people and their elected representatives decide government policy, and federalism, in which the responsibilities of government are divided between federal and provincial governments.

The new dispensation was embodied in the Act of Union, passed on July 23, 1840. By it, Upper and Lower Canada were united into a single province or colony of Canada which, for some purposes such as administration, was then divided in two halves. Technically knows as Canada East and Canada West, the old names of Lower and Upper Canada continued in popular usage. Both halves were given forty members of the Legislative Assembly, or MPP's (for Members of the Provincial Parliament). This was the worst gerrymander in Canadian history, a distortion of reality, and a violation of the principle of fairness, because the population of Lower Canada outnumbered that of Upper Canada by 700,000 to around 500,000. French Catholics were a majority in the new Canada, but they elected a minority of representatives.

The arrangement was deliberately designed to submerge the French Catholics in an English-dominated Assembly, because part of the Lower Canadian representation would be English as would all of Upper Canada's MPP's. On paper it looked like a solution to the problems the French Canadian politicians had allegedly caused their British masters. Politically it was a failure. French Canadians instantly saw the intent of Durham's recommendation, and acted like ethnic groups under siege often do – they united to protect their interests. Though never perfectly united, they tended to vote as a block, so the largest faction in the new Assembly was French Canadian.

In order for the English majority to dominate the French minority, the English had to be united. In fact, they were divided into a number of loose factions with shifting members, interests, leaders and voting patterns. Political parties with clear leadership, policies and discipline had not yet evolved. One faction was the Reformers under Robert Baldwin, but more moderate Reformers tended to follow Sir Francis Hincks. A number of MPP's from south western Ontario gradually formed the Clear Grits, with George Brown as their leader. The Tory remnants from Family Compact days were led by William Draper, later by Sir Allan MacNab. A growing number of moderate Conservatives came to be led by John A. Macdonald. Other moderate Liberals rallied behind Sandfield Macdonald. All of these seven leaders served as chief minister or premier, some for several terms, none for any lengthy period of time.

The first Governor of the new Canada was Charles Thomson, Lord Sydenham, who arrived with instructions to thwart the development of democracy. He was an excellent and experienced politician, and put together a government under Draper that had enough support to address the problems that rebellion had postponed. But he fell off his horse, bumped his head, and died. The largest faction at the time was Baldwin's Reformers. He was a man of great principle but was somewhat inflexible. Hincks, the lesser Reform leader, had fewer principles and more flexibility. He worked out an alliance with the Lower Canadian Reformers under Louis-Hippolyte LaFontaine. In the elections of 1841 the Reformers won a clear majority in both halves of Canada.

The next Governor, Charles Bagot, tried to work with the Reformers, and invited Baldwin and several others to take positions in the Executive Council. They did, but soon discovered that Bagot was determined to rule by himself. Bagot manoeuvred, appointed other ministers, and tried to govern against the wishes of the Assembly. His problem, though, was that the sources of revenue he controlled directly were shrinking, and he needed the support of the Assembly to carry on. He was also ill, and had to let his ministers govern. His successor was equally unsuccessful, and left the day-to-day management of affairs including patronage appointments to the new chief minister. By default, they had created the position of premier and transferred real power from an appointed British Governor to an elected Canadian politician.

At this time Britain was moving towards freer trade which reduced the imperative to control the colonies. London sent out a new Governor, Lord Elgin, with instructions to implement Responsible Government. Elgin asked LaFontaine and Baldwin to form a government. They did, and from then on governments could only remain in office if they commanded a majority in the Assembly. They were, in effect, responsible to the Assembly, and the Assembly was responsible to the people who got to elect or re-elect their MPP's every four years.

Although this battle dominated politics, the government and the politicians did find time to deal with other matters. One of the most important was building canals. These were essential for developing the economy of Upper Canada, but it alone lacked the resources to build them and Lower Canada lacked the incentive. Now a single government presided over the economic and commercial destiny of the entire St. Lawrence-Great Lakes system, and it had the capacity to tax and borrow to complete major improvements to the canal system.

At the same time Canada entered the railway age, and the Canadian government quickly got into the business of supporting railway construction. The Grand Trunk Railway was opened from Toronto to Montreal in1856, extended to Sarnia in the west by 1859 and then to Rivière du Loup on the lower St. Lawrence, a total distance of 1,600 kilometers. A series of lines shot northwards into the Shield from ports on Lakes Ontario and Erie, and more east-west lines crossed from the Ottawa River to Lake Huron. While never having as many railways as the hundreds of little towns demanded, Ontario soon had many more miles of track than the economy could sustain.

The government also tackled administrative reforms. The fight over Clergy Reserves sputtered on for a few more years until John A. Macdonald's government worked out a solution that gave most of the land to the Anglican Church but satisfied the others. Baldwin believed that all levels of government should be responsible to the people. At the municipal level he created elected county, city, township and town governments which were responsible for local government and for raising the taxes to pay for them. In each district the people learned that if they wanted improvements, they had to pay for them, the ultimate basis and test of responsible government. That system has remained intact ever since, subject to a higher and broader level of regional government being added in the 1960s. Little things were not entirely over-looked, as the currency moved from pounds and shillings to dollars and cents.

In Upper Canada a system of government-supported common schools was established under the supervision of the Methodist minister Egerton Ryerson, who managed it for the next 30 years, leaving an indelible imprint on education in Ontario. It was specifically meant to instil Christian religious values and morality. Its supporters assumed that these were "common" values, but the vast majority of the population was Protestant, and Protestants would staff the school boards, provide the teachers and make all the decisions about values, curriculum and textbooks. The public school system was, in effect, a Protestant school system. Catholics viewed it as such, and demanded separate schools where the moral lessons would be taught by Catholics and not Protestants.

With the support of the French Catholic majority in Lower Canada plus Irish and Scottish Catholic MPP's in both Canadas, the government agreed to establish separate schools. They were limited to primary education, to only one religious minority, the Catholics, and to teaching in English or German, but that did not prevent Brown and the Grits condemning the compromise as a sell-out to French Catholics. The question of separate schools would remain a dominant political issue for over a century and has never fully been resolved. The old Tory attempt to create an Anglican provincial university also came to naught when a government-supported secular university, University College, was established in Toronto. Private sectarian universities like Queen's (Presbyterian), McMaster (Baptist), Trinity (Anglican), St. Michaels (Catholic) and Victoria (Methodist) were permitted but not given support.

While these reforms were being implemented, the economy was booming. International conditions were favourable, and exports surged – especially for wheat and square timber, but also for lumber, oats, barley, flour and other foodstuffs. The main market was the United States, and trade expanded even faster after tariffs on raw materials were abolished by the Reciprocity Treaty of 1854. Immigrants from the British Isles poured in by the tens of thousands, pushing the agricultural frontier northwards into less productive land, but creating more demand and producing more goods for consumption and export. Towns and cities flourished, both to house and service the larger population, and to benefit from and contribute to growing prosperity. The industrial revolution was underway, with blacksmith shops evolving into carriage factories, cabinet makers becoming furniture factories, and a myriad of shops producing harness, stoves, tools, china, and cutlery. The farm machinery factories of Hart Massey and John Harris were becoming major exporters.

Behind this economic boom the government performed poorly under the Act of Union. The original hope – that the English majority of MPP's would dominate the French minority – proved impossible from the start. Instead, a system evolved in which governments tried to have a majority of MPPs in both Canadas, an informal "double majority", so that any legislation passed would satisfy both English and French. But while it was always clear which faction had a majority in Lower Canada, it was rarely clear which faction dominated in Upper Canada. Nevertheless, a number of leading politicians tried to put together governments based on majorities from both halves. When that failed the only remaining possibility was governments based on the French Catholic block plus a minority of MPP's from Upper Canada, a situation infuriating to many English Protestants. These governments also proved to be unstable, and from 1854 to 1862 there were six administrations. In the next two years there were four more and two elections.

One of the issues that caused much friction at this time was "representation by population". In 1841 the population of Lower Canada was 200,000 larger than that of Upper Canada. Since the purpose of the union was to swamp the French Canadians, the two halves of the province were both given 40 seats. English Canadians were very pleased with that, and the protests of French Canadians could safely be ignored, or so it was thought. But most immigrants went to Upper Canada, and the census of 1851 gave it a larger population (950,000 to 890,000), a disparity that had grown to 300,000 by 1861. English Canadians now decided that the system was unfair, and seats should be based on population, giving Upper Canada, of course, the larger number. After 20 years of under-representation and political discrimination, no French Canadian MPP could possibly endorse such a change, and no government could make the change without some of their votes.

By the early 1860's it was becoming increasingly clear to most politicians that a new system had to be designed to deal with the stalemate. The initiative surprisingly came from George Brown, previously one of the most intransigent of all politicians. By now the leader of the largest faction in Upper Canada, the Reformers, he proposed in 1864 a Grand Coalition with his enemy, John A. Macdonald, who led the smaller Conservative faction in Upper Canada, and George Étienne Cartier, who led the largest faction in Lower Canada. Their job was to work together on a solution, and the best idea in play was confederation.

Confederation meant that the current unworkable system in Canada would be replaced with a federal system in which a single Canadian government would continue to look after things of interest to the whole of Canada, like railways and defence. The two halves, Upper and Lower Canada, would become distinct provinces, with their own governments to look after issues of local interest, such as education or religion. That way French Canadians would finally escape from the forced assimilation the Union Act was designed to achieve, and Upper Canada would escape from the "dictatorship" of recent governments based on a French majority allied to a minority of Upper Canada MPP's.

Greater possibilities were afoot, however. The governments of the four Atlantic colonies – Nova Scotia, New Brunswick, Newfoundland and Prince Edward Island – were facing problems of small markets and excessive governmental cost. They were planning a meeting to discuss a federation similar to the one being mooted in Canada. They willingly agreed to let a Canadian delegation join them at their proposed meeting in Charlottetown in 1864.

External factors also weighed heavily on the delegates. The United States was suffering through a horrendously bloody civil war, which ended in 1865. The victorious North was in an expansionist mood, had some grudges with Britain, and had and enormous and experienced army. Britain wanted its colonies to take a larger role in their own defence, and that could best be done by a single government. And after the war a number of Irish volunteers attacked Canada to put pressure on Britain to free Ireland. They were never a serious threat, but their small excursions exposed the weaknesses of colonial defences.

Britain also wanted to reduce the overall administrative costs of Empire. Throughout the Confederation debates and afterwards it made its enthusiasm quite clear, pressured and perhaps bribed politicians, and appointed pro-Confederation governors to influence the process. The 1854 Reciprocity Treaty between Canada and the United States was coming up for renewal. Washington was not favourably disposed because the Treaty had worked mainly to the advantage of Canada. The Treaty was cancelled in 1865, leading Canadian merchants to look to the Maritimes as an alternative market.

Finally, an increasing number of dreamers plus a few realists shared a vision of acquiring the western prairies from the Hudson's Bay Company. The vision was driven by the fact that almost all of Upper Canada's good agricultural land had been occupied, and the prairies were needed for the surplus farm population. That development could also provide a new market for the growing industries of Upper Canada. Perhaps British Columbia could also be lured into the federation. By the time the delegates met, the intoxicating idea of a super colony stretching from Atlantic to Pacific was very much alive – all they had to do was figure out how to create a federal union.

Macdonald became one of the prime architects of Confederation, but he did not achieve the type of federation he wanted. His desire was to have a Canadian political structure similar to the British one, with an all-powerful unitary government plus a number of subordinate municipal governments to administer purely local matters like schools and rural roads. The majority of delegates did not agree. French Canadians had no intention of continuing in a political system in which their lives could be dominated by a majority of English Canadians. The Maritime delegates had no intention of having Central Canada dominate them. And a large number of Upper Canadians, possibly a majority, saw in Macdonald's scheme a potential continuation of the system that had so frustrated them, namely a strong central government based on a French Canadian block combined with a minority of Upper Canadians, imposing the views and interests of Montreal and Quebec on Upper Canada.

Macdonald lost the main debate – the new colony would have a federal constitution like the United States, not a unitary one like Britain. The compromise document went to the British Government for consideration. When they decided what form Canada should take, they passed the British North America Act to make it law. It was decided to apply the name Canada to the whole federation and to adopt the existing Canadian capital of Ottawa, including the new Parliament buildings whose scandal-ridden construction was nearing completion.

The British North America Act of 1867 gave the federal government the main source of government revenue, namely customs. Ottawa could also collect both direct and indirect taxes, which gave it great fiscal strength, while the provinces could only collect direct ones, which were quite limited in the nineteenth century. In return for taking over the collection of customs, Ottawa would provide the provinces with a subsidy to cover most provincial costs. The subsidy was based on population, which theoretically took politics out of its administration.

Section 91 of the British North America Act gave the federal government control of matters of broad interest, such as money and banking, the postal services, inter-provincial railroads, rivers and canals, Indian affairs, defence, trade, commerce and foreign affairs, criminal law and the appointment of senior justices. In fact, however, London retained control of defence, trade and foreign affairs though these gradually devolved to the federal government. Ottawa had responsibility for "peace, order and good government" and residual responsibility for new issues that might arise, though by definition that meant little at the time.

Ottawa inherited Britain's power to annul provincial legislation. This power was designed to prevent a colonial assembly passing legislation that threatened the interests of the Empire, and had only been used once in the previous two decades. Ottawa also inherited the right to appoint lieutenant governors for each province, but they had become mere figureheads since the adoption of responsible government. That, in fact, was one of the only powers Britain delegated to Canada in the BNA Act. Canada remained a colony, Queen Victoria remained the sovereign, sovereignty continued to rest in London, the constitution remained a British document, and disputes over it could only be settled by the Judicial Committee of the British Privy Council.

Section 92 of the Act gave the provinces control of matters of provincial and local importance or relevance. That included property and natural resources – agricultural land, forests, minerals and local rivers – the main basis of wealth. The provinces controlled public works like roads, local canals and railroads, civil rights, municipalities, health, welfare, culture, the police, civil law, the lower courts, and the administration of justice. Some of these responsibilities only became important later, such as health and welfare. Education was under provincial control, subject to the protection of Catholic separate schools in Ontario and Protestant separate schools in Quebec. It has often been asserted that "provincial rights" were purely "local" but control of natural resources and the right to build roads from Cornwall to Sault Ste Marie were hardly "local". In 1867 local matters were what mattered to most Canadians. This compromise constitution was then passed by the Upper Canadian MLAs by an overwhelming vote of 54 to eight.

Toronto, the bustling, self-confident manufacturing and financial capital of 50,000, became the provincial capital once more. The decision to adopt the name "Ontario" is somewhat of a mystery, but after some debate a decision was made to adopt the name of the easternmost Great Lake. The former Canada had a dual administration, and part of it was transferred to the new province. On July 1, 1867, Ontario was launched as a province in the federal Dominion of Canada

Chapter Four
Building a Province and Defining Federalism, 1867 – 1896

With the adoption of Confederation, John A. Macdonald became interim Prime Minister of Canada, pending the first election. He appointed the first lieutenant governor of Ontario and asked him to appoint John Sandfield Macdonald as interim premier, a blatant interference in provincial politics. Sandfield was a dour, honest, arbitrary and stubborn Highland Catholic who made enemies easily. He had, however, been premier, and of the experienced politicians in the province he was as good a choice as any.

Both provincial and federal elections were held on the same day. Sandfield led a loose group of Reformers and Conservatives; John A. led his Liberal-Conservatives. Candidates could run both federally and provincially, and some of them were elected to both houses. The two Macdonalds cooperated in the selection of candidates, and campaigned together. They both won, Sandfield with 50 out of 82 seats. They then set out to govern Canada and Ontario as they thought it should be governed – with a strong central government and a weak provincial one. Sandfield immediately adopted a subordinate position, even sending John A. drafts of Ontario legislation for approval.

For a man who saw himself as the reeve of a huge municipality, Sandfield certainly acted like a bona fide premier. Freed from the paralysis and instability of the Union, Sandfield's regime forged ahead with a series of reforms in education, reforming primary and secondary education, making it free for everyone, and improving the qualifications of teachers. It founded a Technical College, and the School of Agriculture, which became the University of Guelph. It put the taxation of timber-cutting rights on a sound basis, and revenue poured into the province's coffers. Mining regulations were upgraded and made uniform, and claims were revoked if not developed.

Sandfield encouraged immigration from Britain, providing assistance with passage, free land and implements to new settlers, and subsidizing colonization roads and railways into the Muskoka, Haliburton and Parry Sound districts. An indication of its activity is the fact that government spending jumped 50% in four years. As such it could still not consume the huge federal subsidies Ontario received from the Confederation agreements. In 1871 Sandfield gave subsidies to railways that almost equalled the annual budget, and the remaining surplus was still over twice the annual expenditure.

The alliance with John A. was not successful. John A's majority rested heavily on Quebec, and he had to make a number of decisions that seemed to favour French and Catholics, to the great displeasure of Ontario's English Protestant majority. Sandfield had to support John A, and was therefore seen as his lackey. The enormous grants to railways were announced without debate in the Assembly, which invited accusations of corruption. Sandfield almost lost his majority in the 1871 election. Old, sick, and dispirited, he met the Assembly, lost several votes, and resigned.

The man who bested him was a brilliant 34-year old lawyer, Edward Blake. He abolished the system under which politicians could sit in both provincial and federal assemblies, and then opted for Ottawa. Blake was replaced by Oliver Mowat, a highly-intelligent, sincere, sober, religious, honest and dull man. He was also a shrewd and careful politician, a good listener, and an excellent decision-maker. He had been highly successful at law, and did much of the drafting of Sections 91 and 92 of the BNA Act. Mowat would be premier for the next 24 years, the most successful politician in Ontario's history, one of the best ever in Canada.

The province's third premier immediately made his mark by solving a major problem created when a previous government had made it too easy for municipalities to sell bonds to support railway construction. Many of them had abused the power, and drifted towards bankruptcy as a result. Mowat could not allow that to happen, but he did not want to reward incompetence or insult the well-governed municipalities. His solution was to give all municipalities $2.00 per capita – the ones in difficulty could pay off their debts, the others could use it as they chose. As a result, thousands of schools, courthouses, town halls, parks, hospitals and libraries were built, and can still be seen throughout the province.

Paradoxically, economic development slowed after 1867 even though Confederation solved some economic problems. The whole of Canada became a single market, Canada acquired the prairies, and a transcontinental railway was completed in 1885. The west did serve as a colony for Ontario's surplus rural population, and Manitoba became a child of Ontario economically, politically and culturally. However, the rate of population growth slowed dramatically. Emigration to the west and the United States exceeded immigration into the province and overall growth was less than the natural increase in a province with a high birth rate

Declining immigration meant that the proportion of the population born in Ontario rose from 70% in 1871 to 82% in 1901. More immigrants came from England and fewer from Scotland and Ireland. Ontario's "Englishness" became more visible, and US influence dwindled as Americans became a smaller minority and were assimilated into English-Canadian society. In eastern Ontario migration from Quebec gradually increased the province's French Canadian population. That migration followed the old canoe routes leaving northern Ontario with a large French population.

Despite the lower rate of growth, the economy did develop and diversify. Wheat no longer held its attraction in the British and American markets, and farmers diversified into barley, oats, corn, tobacco, fruit, cattle and the dairy industry. The government continued to encourage settlement in northern Ontario, a policy that cost great sums of money and achieved little other than hardship for farmers struggling to carve homesteads out of land suited for growing trees. North of a line from Kingston to Georgian Bay, Ontario remains dotted with the foundations of farm buildings and the piles of stones poor farmers once dug by hand from infertile soil.

Lumber, however, was a booming industry, pushing steadily into the Precambrian Shield, and yielding enormous riches and substantial government revenues. The government gradually tightened regulations, increased taxes, and provided forest fire protection. The largest nickel deposits in the world were discovered at Sudbury in 1883, along with iron near Sault Ste Marie and silver at Cobalt. Hamilton, with its superb harbour and easy access to American coal, developed an iron and steel industry to feed the new industrialization. In the 1890s hydro-electricity was developed at Sault Ste Marie for the pulp and paper plant, and in 1892 the Canadian Niagara Power Company was established.

In the south the advent of farm machinery meant that less labour was required per acre, and rural depopulation became a huge social and political issue. Some counties experied a 50% decline in population in the last three decades of the century. Rural population shrank from 75% of the province in 1871 to 55% in 1901. In the cities and towns, economic expansion was continuous, with new factories springing up and new streets pressing into the surrounding countryside. Toronto grew from 50,000 at Confederation to 200,000 at the turn of the century. In the big cities, tramways and railways moved workers between the suburbs and city centres. A revolution was also underway in communications when phones became common, and electricity changed forever the functioning of factories and mines and the lives of city folk.

The economic slowdown occurred in spite of the government's efforts. Mowat was fully aware that his key constituency was the farmer, and the government assisted agriculture with drainage, marketing, transportation, education, weed control, agricultural schools, and a Department of Agriculture in 1888. At the federal level, John A. Macdonald's National Policy of 1878 raised tariffs so that domestic manufactured goods were competitive with imports. Consumers from coast to coast bought Canadian manufacturers, and most of those goods came from Ontario. At the same time, the provincial government began regulating the worst abuses of industrialization, mining and forestry, with laws on minimum age, safety, sanitation, workman's compensation, the rights of labour organizations, and the establishment of Labour Day.

It was in this period that small town Ontario took its present form. Two and three story brick stores line a four-lane main street, housing all the stores a town needs. Banks are more likely to be made of stone, but carved stone often graces the brick stores. Farther along main street and on the streets running back from it are situated the beautiful churches with their distinctive architecture, stained-glass windows and tall spires. Beside wide tree-lined streets stood the houses of the rich and the middle class, often three stories, with room for families of six or eight plus servants.

An ornate railway station would be an important centre of activity half a dozen times a day, and the tracks might set off the poorer district, past the lumber yard, livery stable, coal yard, grain elevator, and perhaps stock yards. At one end of town, or near the mill, factories were appearing, five or six stories high, to manufacture all manner of goods. Somewhere along the stream there would be a park, where a band would play on Sundays, and there might be a place for the new and popular sport of baseball. On the edge of town would be the fair grounds where once a year the farmers gathered to compete for prizes. It usually included a course for horse racing. Towns would have a Masonic Lodge and an Orange Lodge, a skating and curling rink, and several other community buildings. And here and there would be inns and hotels of varying quality, catering to customers of varying quality.

Mowat was the first Ontario premier to face the vexing problem of prohibition. Excessive drinking, alcohol abuse, physical abuse of relatives, broken families, fist-fights, accidents, death and loss of farm or job were endemic to nineteenth-century Ontario. Liquor was the popular answer to physical and emotional hardship, illness, loneliness, and the discomfort of travel, and there was one inn for every 70 adult males. In mid-century the temperance movement arose to deal with these abuses. It soon turned into a movement to prohibit any consumption of alcohol, a crusade for the perfection of mankind. It was essentially a militant British Protestant movement. It failed to achieve much success by teaching, preaching and moral suasion, so it demanded that government make it illegal for anyone to produce or consume alcohol. The goal was to use government to impose religious values on everyone, especially non church-goers, fallen Christians, urban workers, immigrants and Catholics.

Mowat, an abstainer, thought that drinking was a matter of personal choice. He did not believe government could or should impose prohibition. However, as the movement grew in strength, he had no option but to respond, though in the slowest and smallest ways possible. He set up the first of many commissions to study the matter, giving them ample time to complete the task. The province took over the administration of inns from the municipalities, and reduced the number of drinking establishments from 6,000 to 4,000. That also allowed Mowat to create a huge patronage network of innkeepers and inspectors. In 1884 he raised the minimum drinking age to 16, and in 1890 to 18, and every year saw an increase in licence fees or a decrease in the number of licences. Consumption and abuse both fell enough for Mowat to retain the support of many prohibitionists, but slowly enough for him to retain the support of the liquor interests as well.

Religious convictions also made education a difficult problem to manage. Protestants insisted that the "public" school system was secular, but the school day began with the recitation of the Lord's Prayer, a clear contradiction of secular status. The school boards and teachers were Protestant, and they and the public insisted that schools teach moral values. They argued that such values were common, but they were, in fact, Protestant values, and Catholics saw them as such. That fact created a clear justification for Catholic schools which, in Catholic eyes, were no more Catholic than the "public" schools were Protestant. The Minister of Education even had a book of scriptures prepared for compulsory reading in the allegedly secular schools. That produced heated debate, and the government's book of scriptures was withdrawn.

Mowat was also the first premier to be challenged by the intractable problem of language in the schools. While English was the language of most schools,

German, Gaelic and French were used in some districts because those were the languages of the teachers and the students. The English assumed that these second languages would disappear as people were assimilated, and that happened in the German and Gaelic areas. But in the Ottawa Valley more schools, both public and Catholic, switched to French due to migration from Quebec.

Protestant militants like the members of the Orange Lodge saw this as part of a Catholic conspiracy to swamp their civilization, and demanded the use of English only and the abolition of all separate schools. Irish Catholics were also increasingly concerned, because the quality of the French teachers was very low, giving the Irish a choice between poor French Catholic teachers or good English Protestant ones. And all Catholics had legitimate grievances – separate schools covered only the primary grades, and a considerable portion of Catholic property taxes was being diverted to the public schools.

This was a no-win situation for the government, because separate schools were guaranteed under the BNA Act and the only teachers available in much of eastern Ontario were poorly-qualified French Canadians. Mowat appointed a number of commissions to study the problems. They revealed that the quality of teaching was, indeed, very low, that French texts were being used, that Catholicism was creeping into the curriculum in a few public schools, and that students were graduating who spoke only French. The government's response was to ensure that more Catholic tax money went to the separate schools, to improve the training and raise the qualifications of French teachers, to standardize the curricula, and to require the teaching of English in French schools.

Mowat's greatest achievement was in defining for the whole of Canada what federalism really meant, and he has been rightly identified as the Father of Provincial Rights. The first skirmish with Ottawa was over the appointment of Queen's Counsels, a patronage plum for Liberal or Conservative governments to give to loyal supporters in the legal profession. Previously they had been appointed by the Governor-in-Council on the advice of the premier, so the question after 1867 was whether that meant the government in Ottawa or in Toronto. Prime Minister Macdonald argued that it was the central government, but Mowat passed legislation affirming that Ontario had always had the power and had not given it up. Ontario retained the right, and Mowat won round one.

The second skirmish was over which level of government inherited an estate when someone died without a will (escheats). Mowat argued that before Confederation, Upper Canada was sovereign in this matter, and had not surrendered that sovereignty in 1867. Ottawa argued that since the subject of escheats was not mentioned in the BNA Act, it was residual, and therefore Ottawa's. While the amount involved was small, the implications were enormous – Mowat was arguing that both federal and provincial governments were fully sovereign within their respective areas of responsibility. The question was appealed to the Judicial Committee of the Privy Council (JCPC) in London, the highest court in the British Empire and hence the ultimate authority on the interpretation of British legislation such as the BNA Act. It found for Ontario.

Mowat's next victory was his biggest, with profound implications for the shape of Canada and of federalism, namely the Ontario-Manitoba border dispute. Ontario's northern and western borders had not been demarcated at the time of Confederation, and those of the new Manitoba of 1870 extended only a few miles north and east of Winnipeg. With settlers and prospectors moving into the area in between, jurisdiction had to be determined. Ottawa proposed a border just east of Fort William (Thunder Bay), running north to the watershed of Hudson Bay and James Bay, and eastwards along that watershed to Quebec, with Manitoba getting everything to the north and west.

Ontario was outraged. The 1763 border between Upper Canada and the United States ran from Fort William to Lake of the Woods, and Ontario accordingly claimed Lake of the Woods as its western border, with the line running straight north to Hudson Bay. In the early 1880s both provinces sent police to "their" region, the police arrested each other, and two provincial elections were held on the same day. But no one was killed in this so-called Battle of Rat Portage, now Kenora.

The federal proposal would have given Manitoba half of modern-day Ontario and rendered Ontario the fourth largest province, after Quebec, BC, and Manitoba, an intolerable affront to the people who saw themselves as the nation's natural leaders. That, however, was not the only issue. The BNA Act gave natural resources to the provinces, but Macdonald violated that understanding by retaining control of resources when Manitoba was created. In proposing to extend Manitoba's borders all the way to Quebec, Ottawa was trying to keep control of a vast stretch of valuable timber and potential mineral wealth. Manitoba would have the administrative burden; Ottawa would have control and the revenue. Keeping control of Manitoba's resources backfired, as Manitoba did not lend much support to Ottawa's position.

Premier Mowat saw this issue as of such importance that he threatened to separate Ontario from Canada if the federal government did not deal fairly and justly with the provinces. Confederation could not survive, he asserted, if provincial rights were subject to the whims of every federal ministry. The issue finally went to the JCPC in London, and it sided with Ontario. One result was that Ontario would permanently have the size, population, wealth and confidence to stand up to Ottawa on constitutional disputes.

Another dispute broke out over the control of rivers inside Ontario. A certain Peter MacLaren had built a timber slide on the Mississippi River, a tributary of the Ottawa River, and would not let others use it. Ontario could not allow an individual to prevent all lumbering upstream just by building a timber slide. The government proposed legislation stating that anyone could use such facilities in return for a fair fee to be established by the government. Ottawa disallowed the legislation on the grounds that it violated MacLaren's "private rights", which were a federal responsibility. Mowat replied that the dam was on provincial crown land, and Ottawa could only disallow such legislation if it threatened the overall interests of Canada, which this clearly did not. Ontario passed its legislation again. Ottawa disallowed it again. Ontario passed it again, and Ottawa disallowed it for the third time. The case then went to the JCPC in London, and once more it found for Mowat, victory number four.

The next dispute was over the meaning of the word "local", the BNA Act having given the provinces control of local issues. The issue was control of licences to sell liquor, a massive industry with 4,000 inns dispensing the devil's brew. By the political mores of the day, an inn keeper in a Liberal province who wanted to obtain a licence would be expected to be a Liberal supporter, to say good things about the Liberals to his customers, and to help get the local Liberal re-elected. Now, with a new federal layer of government, and a Conservative one at that, issuing licences and controlling patronage became vitally important for both the provincial Liberals and the federal Conservatives.

For a while both levels of government appointed inspectors and tried to control the trade. Ontario argued that the licensing of inns was a local matter, and hence provincial; Ottawa argued that selling liquor was commerce, and therefore federal. When this case finally came to JCPC, it decreed that the federal government's control of commerce related to national issues. Liquor licences were clearly local, and Macdonald had lost the battle to define local as national.

Mowat won three more battles over the constitution. Both governments attempted to regulate insurance companies. Mowat argued that provincial authority over property and civil rights was more important than federal responsibility for commerce – again the JCPC supported Ontario. Two more battles related to the tactics Ottawa was using in these disputes. At Confederation, Ottawa inherited from London the right to appoint provincial lieutenant governors. Macdonald saw them as instruments of federal power, his own lieutenants, men who could influence provincial governments and exercise a governor's power to refuse to sign legislation or to reserve it for Ottawa's judgment. These powers had gone into disuse with the granting of responsible government. After two decades of battle, Ontario's lieutenant governors reverted to the figure-head status that their predecessors had held in the two decades before Confederation.

The BNA act had also transferred to Ottawa London's right to disallow provincial legislation. Macdonald saw this as another instrument for asserting federal power over the provinces, and reserved 22 provincial laws in the first four years alone. Mowat argued before the JCPC that this rule was designed to prevent colonies passing legislation clearly harmful to the overall interests of Canada, not to assert central control over local issues. That is how London had used the power, disallowing only one colonial act in British North America in the 25 years before Confederation. Again the JCPC agreed with Mowat, and the federal government had to stop abusing the right of disallowance.

While Canada developed into a true federation, Ontario moved closer to democracy. In the elections of 1871 everyone voted on the same day for the first time, and property owners were allowed to vote in only one constituency. Property qualifications were gradually reduced until there was universal adult male suffrage by 1888. The secret ballot was introduced in provincial, municipal and school board elections in 1875. Women had the vote in municipal elections but would have to struggle for another 40 years to win the vote provincially. In the 1890s the duly-elected politicians also obtained a new home in the modern Legislative Buildings, whose name, Queen's Park, soon became synonymous with the Ontario Government.

Mowat proved to be an enormously successful politician, winning six consecutive elections. He defeated every challenge posed by the Opposition, the government in Ottawa, and a number of thorny issues like prohibition and separate schools. He appointed good men to his Cabinet, allowed them to administer their departments, supported them, and renewed personnel when necessary. His government was widely representative of the regions, of town and country, and of the various religions including Catholics. He also used patronage masterfully.

When demand grew for new institutions or policies, Mowat monitored the issue, set up a commission to study it in detail, and watched the Opposition in case they developed policies he could steal. He waited for public opinion to reach a critical mass, and then introduced the minimal amount of change required. If there was still pressure to do more, he would tighten or expand the regulations. He was, in fact, a conservative thinker, a moderate reformer, a pragmatist, and a man with his hand firmly on the pulse of Ontario.

His political success, however, was not quite what the election results suggest. In four of the six elections that he won, the Liberals outvoted the Conservatives by around 1%. These close votes came in spite of the fact that he controlled patronage, the dates of elections and the government agenda. He could attract good candidates with guarantees of jobs, had a budget surplus until the 1890s, presided over a province that was growing, and had an easy foil in the Conservative government in Ottawa which he regularly bested on a number of issues.

The fact is that once in power, it was relatively easy for a government to win re-election by gerrymandering, the practice of drawing constituency boundaries to favour government candidates. It was highly undemocratic, a violation of the principle of representation by population which Upper Canada had fought for two decades to obtain. All governments did it, and Mowat was one of the best, repeatedly converting around 48% of the popular vote into 2/3 of the Assembly seats. He played other tricks on the electorate, one of them being to make farmers' sons eligible to vote on the grounds that agriculture was a virtuous vocation! In spite of this, he still deserved to win because of his excellent management of a number of difficult problems and his progressive policies on the full range of issues. In short, Mowat caught the mood of Ontario. In 1896 he joined the new Liberal Government in Ottawa, leaving his successor a well-managed province and a superb political machine.

Chapter Five
Boom Time and War Time, 1896 – 1918

The turn of the century witnessed profound change in Ontario. One of the greatest economic booms in world history put an end to three decades of slow growth, recession and stagnation. Almost all the conditions that had retarded the opening of the Canadian prairies changed, and spectacular growth there provided a huge market for Ontario's industries. The United States and Europe experienced unprecedented prosperity, creating further demand for Ontario's exports. Cheap and abundant capital poured in to finance new mines, industries, buildings and transportation facilities.

The economy was also changing. Electricity began to replace water power in factories and mines, and to replace manpower in farms, stores and houses. Trucks and tractors were replacing horses on the farm and in transportation. Ford opened a factory in Windsor in 1904; GM opened one in Oshawa in 1908. A network of hard-surfaced provincial roads began to appear. Eaton's and Simpson's provided a vast array of products from their stores or through mail-order. Some city dwellers came to enjoy running water, adequate sewage, and the luxury of electricity, though slums were still common where life was cold, dark, cramped, and unhealthy.

Limited economic prospects and deteriorating political conditions in England and Europe prompted millions to immigrate. Some came to Ontario, whose population grew by 300,000 in the decade following 2000 compared to only 100,000 in the previous decade. These gains were not as large as natural increase – Ontario's young were migrating, and its proportion of Canada's population was shrinking quickly. Urbanization and rural depopulation were accelerating, the rural population declining from 60% in 1891 to 45% in 1911. Toronto alone gained as many people as did the whole province. The ethnic mix continued to evolve as most immigrants came from Great Britain, and migration from Quebec increased the French population from 5% to 10%.

The economic boom was a godsend for the Liberal regime, because old age was clearly visible in its handling of issues or, more often, in its failure to handle them. Although the province's fourth premier, Arthur Hardy, was a capable minister, he was also old and ill. He struggled to win the 1898 election, the Liberal's eighth in a row, but with the same number of seats as in 1894. Liberal popular support fell, the party had to resort to even more tricks and gerrymanders to retain power, and a strong whiff of scandal was in the air.

One major achievement, however, was to make it illegal to export logs to the United States, resulting in a boom in the saw milling industry, the creation of thousands of jobs, and a jump in the value-added of Ontario's exports. In 1913 the government applied the same policy to pulp wood, resulting in massive American investment in pulp and paper plants from the Ottawa Valley to Dryden. During World War I, INCO was finally coerced into refining nickel in Ontario, as the export mix shifted from raw materials to refined resources, creating more investment and jobs in the province.

Premier Hardy's successor, George Ross, had been Minister of Education for 16 years, but still had some imagination and energy. However, he mishandled the key political issue – prohibition. For three decades a growing number of prohibitionists had been demanding a total ban on the manufacture and sale of alcohol. Ross was a prohibitionist, but when he called for yet another study instead of action, the prohibitionists felt betrayed. The Conservatives had finally obtained effective leadership in James Whitney. He had greatly weakened the influence of extreme Protestant Orangemen in the party and recruited several prominent French Catholics. Throughout the Mowat years the Conservatives had actually been more progressive on many issues, but the people preferred to see the reliable Mowat government implement those proposals. Whitney was not only progressive, but he and his team started to look a lot better than the stumbling Liberals.

For years the Conservatives had dominated the cities, and the rapid growth of populations and the resulting increase in the number of urban seats coupled with rural depopulation in Liberal areas favoured the Conservatives. In addition, having a Liberal government in Ottawa was a problem for the provincial Liberals. The new federal Prime Minister, Wilfrid Laurier, insisted that Hardy appoint a French Canadian as Speaker of the Assembly in order to solidify Liberal support for both provincial and federal parties. Hardy reluctantly yielded to the pressure, but it did not stop the erosion of French support. It also gave the opposition the argument that if the province wanted to be governed from Toronto rather than Ottawa, it had best elect a Conservative government.

In the election of 1902 the Conservatives actually outpolled the Liberals by 50.2% to 47.5%, but clever alterations to constituency borders gave the Liberals 50 seats to 48 for the Tories. In addition to gerrymandering and the generous distribution of patronage and liquor, the Liberals had engaged in outright vote rigging. In Sault Ste Marie they had brought a boatload of Americans across the river, arranged for them to vote several times, got them drunk and sent them home. At the time of the election the major employer in the city was almost bankrupt and had laid off thousands of workers. The government stepped in, saved the company, and paid off the workers. That looked a bit like bribery.

On the first day of the new legislative session, one of the biggest scandals in Ontario's history rocked the province. The Liberal majority was shaky, but it gained a seat when R.R. Gamey crossed the floor, stating that he was joining the government to get economic development for his constituency. Immediately after the Speech from the Throne, he announced that he had been bribed, crossed back to the Conservative side, and handed a surprised Whitney an envelope with the relevant documents and $500 of the $1,500 he had allegedly been paid. Shock waves swept through the stunned Assembly, the accused Minister turned pale, the Opposition demanded an investigation by a committee of MPPs, journalists rushed to get the story out, and a crowd of people started streaming towards Queen's Park to see the action. The government had its way in appointing a small judicial enquiry, and it found what it was supposed to – that Gamey was a liar and the government was innocent. Few people were likely to believe that, and the government drifted towards certain defeat in the 1905 election.

There was a swing of about 3% from Liberals to Conservatives, making it the first government in Ontario's history to actually win a majority of the popular vote. The disparity in constituency size and the first-past-the-post system now worked to the Conservatives' advantage, resulting in 69 seats to the Liberals 50. Whitney had been an excellent Leader of the Opposition, attracting a strong team representing all regions, the different races and religions, farmers, workers and professionals, and developing good policies. He proved to be even better in the premier's job, and he swept to re-election with 86 seats in 1908, with 82 in 1911, and with 84 in 1914, each victory based on over 50% of the popular vote and without a hint of scandal.

James Pliney Whitney came from the small town of Morrisburg on the St. Lawrence, an area of mixed Loyalist, Scottish and French settlement. It tended to produce two types of people – Protestants and Catholics who hated each other, and ones that got along. Whitney was of the latter group, a factor of profound importance for the re-building of the Conservative Party and in his handling of issues as premier. This was an area where wets predominated, that is those who drank or tolerated drinking, unlike southwest Ontario, the bedrock of both Liberal and prohibitionist politics. Whitney was a heavy drinker in his younger years, and had little tolerance for Christian extremists who tried to use government to force their values on others. He was also tall, handsome, honest, confident, pragmatic, open-minded, and decisive, a strong speaker, good thinker, and an excellent leader, organizer, conciliator and manager.

One of the things that had bothered him during his years in Opposition was the administrative and financial mess at the University of Toronto. This was not a popular issue as only a privileged minority went to university. Still, no province could be great if it lacked a proper university system. Whitney immediately increased the university's funding and put it on a solid footing. He appointed a number of respected experts to make a thorough study of the university, and adopted most of their recommendations. A Board was appointed to govern the University. He appointed the best men available to the Board, and they selected a competent President. This was the first example of Whitney putting into effect the slogan he had used in his speeches: "We are bold enough to be honest; we are honest enough to be bold."

Whitney was not, however, a reformer or even a man of great vision. In most areas of government he simply took existing policies and modified or updated them as circumstances warranted. Thus the province saw steady improvements to health, safety and environmental regulations in industry, mining, forestry and farming. Taxes on mining and lumbering were gradually increased, and the government supported economic development while balancing its budget. Boards were established to manage municipal railways and workman's compensation. Government appointed the members, but they were then relatively free of political interference. Some democratic reforms included making ballots truly secret and preventing MPPs from rushing private members' bills through the Assembly. Whitney cut in half the costs of school texts – for years he had accused the Liberals of giving inflated contracts to friends in the publishing industry. Every household benefited from this measure, and it reinforced his reputation for honesty, for caring, and for honouring promises.

Whitney was a pragmatist on the question of government intervention in the economy. The previous government had started building the Temiskaming and Northern Ontario Railway from North Bay to the Clay Belt, a venture that would open the huge region for settlement, lumbering and mineral exploitation. In opposition Whitney had argued that it should be left to private enterprise, but after the election he simply continued on with it. In 1906 the government bought a mine; three years later it sold it leaving all mining in private hands. There was, in fact, no need for government ownership because mining was booming in northern Ontario, and financing it helped make Toronto's Bay Street a rival to Montreal as Canada's financial capital.

The great achievement of the Whitney Government was the establishment of Ontario Hydro, the world's first publicly-owned power company. Hydro-electricity had been developing rapidly in the late nineteenth century as factories, mines and mills switched to hydro, as more inventions were made and adopted, and as cities built electric tramways. Every municipality wanted access to hydro, for its existing industry, to attract more development, for stores, street lighting, and houses. These were small markets and required investment in transmission lines, and the big American-owned companies at Niagara Falls were not prepared to service them. The stage was set for a classic showdown between the needs of the public and the philosophy and rights of private enterprise.

Whitney provided decisive, energetic, and pragmatic leadership. The greatest champion of hydro electricity in the province was Adam Beck, mayor of London. Whitney brought him into the Cabinet in 1905. Whitney then appointed a commission to study all aspects of electricity. Its outcome was never in doubt, because he appointed Beck to head it, gave him a wide mandate, and provided full support when private companies tried to sabotage the enquiry. The commission duly reported that a government-owned utility should be set up with all the powers needed to produce, transmit, distribute and sell electricity, and expropriate any land or company necessary to achieve that mandate. Business supported the recommendations, and the government immediately accepted them. Beck became both Minister responsible and chairman of the commission.

The big American hydro companies and some small Canadian ones were well aware of the role electricity would play in the future economy of Ontario, and of the enormous profits to be made by a monopoly supplier of a service no industry, store, or house could do without. They fought the government in the courts, in the media, in public opinion, in the political arena, amongst investors, and with appeals to Ottawa. They lost, because Whitney had made up his mind, and Beck was his man. With that kind of support, Beck developed electricity at Niagara Falls, built transmission lines across southern Ontario, built or took over power plants all over the province, and made cheap electricity the foundation of the modern Ontario economy. Beck himself was a man of enormous drive, ambition, energy, imagination, ability, and ruthlessness, with an ego to match, and it took a man of Whitney's character, judgment and strength to give him the support he needed and to control him when necessary.

Whitney's policy towards prohibition was largely the same as Mowat's. He did not believe it could be enforced, and did not like religious extremists who had no sense of Christian charity or tolerance, one-issue citizens with one simple solution, as he saw them. Accordingly, his approach was to do as little as possible. He appointed Conservatives as liquor inspectors because he understood patronage, but he also pointed out that they were imposing government policy for which his government was responsible. He increased the number of inspectors, selected good ones, ordered them to enforce the laws, and did not interfere with them. The cost of licences was increased, sales to minors tightened up again, and the sale of liquor on Sunday was banned.

One controversial change was the requirement for 60% of the voters on a referendum to make a wet municipality dry or vice versa. Whitney believed that with opinion so evenly balanced, a 50% vote could lead to municipalities changing policy at every election. But if the drys got 60% support, the municipality would stay dry, at least until the wets could muster 60% to change it back. The prohibitionists protested, but the number of dry municipalities continued to increase – from 252 out of 844 in 1906 to 440 in 1912 and 502 in 1914. While the cities remained wet, liquor became harder and harder to obtain in Ontario the Good.

The problem of French language rights came to a head in 1912. It was a no-win situation for any government. The English majority wanted the province to be English speaking, and they assumed that all students leaving school would be English-speaking or bilingual. In the Ottawa Valley, the growing French-Canadian minority wanted to retain their French language and Catholic culture, and they were increasingly strident in their demands. They believed they had the right to use French because English Protestant separate schools were protected in Quebec. They wanted French secondary schools, normal schools and the recognition of Quebec teaching qualifications. Minority language education was not, however, a constitutional right in Ontario, simply a fact-of-life since the first settlement, and one which the English expected to disappear with the passage of time. The vast majority of separate Catholic schools were, in fact, for English-speaking Irishmen, and they saw the growing use of French as a threat to the proper education of their children.

Whitney approached the problem the same way Mowat had done – he commissioned studies in order to get the facts, to publicize the issues, to prepare public opinion for change, and to delay any decisions. The commissions found conditions in the separate schools in eastern Ontario almost exactly as they had been 30 years earlier, namely, low funding, low standards, poorly-qualified teachers, numerous unilingual French schools, the use of unauthorized texts, and the teaching of some religion in public schools. Statistically the problem was insignificant, affecting around 200 of 6,000 schools. Politically it was unsolvable – any concession to the French language would be intolerable to Protestants; any move to reduce French instruction would be unacceptable to the French.

Whitney did not share the anti-Catholic, anti-French bias of many of his English Protestant compatriots, and had sent his daughter to a French Catholic school. Indeed, he had turned his back on the Orange extremists and assiduously cultivated French Catholics, making one of their leaders the first French Cabinet Minister to supervise a ministry. This was not an issue on which he was going to bow to Protestant extremists, but nor would he bow to French Canadian nationalism.

He was determined that the educational system would not be divided again, to create a third system based on nationality and language. Schools must produce students who spoke English, who could survive and prosper in an English-speaking environment. That, to him, was manifestly in the interests of all Franco-Ontarians. In June, 1912, the government issued Regulation 17: English was to be the main language of instruction after Grade I, unless students could not understand it. In that case, French could be used for another two years, but not at all after Grade III. The salaries of teachers would be increased and the costs of textbooks reduced, but there would be no provincial support for any school that did not teach in English after Grade III.

Both the Liberal Opposition and English-speaking Catholics approved Regulation 17, so Whitney was surprised when it touched off a firestorm of protest in eastern Ontario, in Quebec, and in federal politics. It was seen by the French as an attack on their culture and the survival of their race. Protests erupted in the Ottawa Valley, teachers resigned, thousands of parents refused to send their children to school, and politicians in Quebec and Ottawa condemned it. Whitney refused to create a third school system based on nationality, but he did agree to slow the rate of implementation. Actually, he had no choice because unilingual French teachers simply could not teach classes in English. The rules were modified to allow French instruction past Grade III for students who could not yet learn in English. No one was satisfied with the outcome, and Regulation 17 would trouble successive regimes for decades.

Whitney had more success on the old question of the province's borders. He had helped his Conservative friend, Robert Borden, win the federal election of 1911. With Conservatives in charge of Manitoba, Ontario and Ottawa, it was time to settle the last border issue – who owned the land north of the Great Lakes watershed. Ontario's opening position was for a line from Lake of the Woods to the Churchill River, and down it to Hudson Bay. Manitoba naturally favoured a line much farther east. The compromise line in the middle was satisfactory to everyone, and Ontario's land mass increased by over 50%. That gave it 600 miles of shoreline on Hudson Bay and James Bay, a vast amount of forest and mineral wealth, and a potential ocean port at Moosonee which was, in fact, linked to North Bay by rail in 1934.

In August, 1914, Britain declared war on Germany, following years of diplomatic skirmishing and rising tensions. As a British colony, Canada was automatically at war, but being semi-independent, it could determine the amount of its contribution. Britain did not have to worry. Ontario was overwhelmingly British and contained a large number of British-born immigrants, and it threw itself enthusiastically into the war. That was fully predictable, as in the decade before the war armouries had been built in every middle-sized town, and young men had signed up in droves to train in them. The government immediately sent London a huge gift of flour, and militias were soon turned into regiments, ready for shipment to the western front in France. Sixty-eight thousand Ontarians were killed or wounded, tens of thousands more suffered deep psychological scars, and every village and town eventually had a war memorial with depressingly long lists of its sacrifices. Many came back heroes, like Billy Bishop, the greatest Allied air ace.

Shortly after war began, the aging Whitney died. Like the Liberals after Mowat's departure, there was no one in the Conservative government of his stature and ability. The seventh premier would be William Hearst, the able and energetic Minister of Lands. Hearst was honest, rigid, difficult to work with, self-confident, self righteous and a prohibitionist, a good partner for Whitney but not a good replacement. His lack of judgment surfaced when he, an MPP from northern Ontario, kept the Agricultural portfolio. That would be a mistake at the best of times – it was a disaster in a province where disgruntled farmers still made up almost half the population and were over-represented in the Assembly. One of them accused Hearst of addressing farm problems with "a diarrhoea of blather and a constipation of help". He was unlucky, too, governing during a war which exaggerated old problems and created new ones.

One new problem was that German Ontarians were now seen as of doubtful loyalty even though some of their families had been Loyalists. They were ostracized, lost their positions as teachers and professors, and Berlin was renamed Kitchener in honour of the top British general. Other "aliens", immigrants born in Germany and the Austro-Hungarian Empire, were imprisoned for the duration of the war.

In all, 240,000 men enlisted, 10% of the entire Ontario population, a staggering rate of about one third of the men of military age. That soon ended the unemployment that had accompanied the recession of 1913, and labour shortages soon affected the entire economy as wartime demand arose for food, lumber, clothing, and above all the instruments of war – artillery, shells, ships, uniforms, boots, and trucks. Ontario's industries were re-tooled, and the province was soon a major supplier of Allied war materiel. The output of mines and lumber camps doubled. Women took the place of men in stores, banks, the professions, and industry – they had always worked just as hard as men on the farm. Boys were excused from school to do more work on farms, but an acute labour shortage soon arose in agriculture.

The government and the opposition threw themselves into the prosecution of the war, and into maximizing Ontario's contribution to it. In this they reflected the view of the vast majority of the province whose motto, adopted in 1909, was "Loyal She Began; Loyal She Remains". As the war ground on year after year, with frightening carnage in the trenches of France and Flanders, as newspapers listed hundreds and then thousands of casualties, and as the demand for more recruits mounted, problems began to emerge in Ontario's war effort. The main one was declining recruitment as the province simply ran out of volunteers to feed the war machine. The federal Conservative government began moving towards conscription, with the full support of the Ontario's MPPs.

Two large groups in Ontario did not agree with conscription – farmers and French Canadians. For the latter, the war was a British affair – they had no love for France and did not in any way see Canada as being threatened. By 1917 any surplus farm boys had long since volunteered. Conscripting made no sense, and farmers demanded exemption from it. Conscription thus created deep divisions between English and French, between urban and rural, and between farmers and both levels of government and both political parties.

Problems also arose in the factories. As governments competed with each other to buy scarce products, prices rose and inflation became a serious problem. Wages rose more slowly, and workers became poorer. But government did nothing to control profits, and share-holders grew richer and company owners amassed fortunes. The shrinking labour force was also under pressure to produce more per worker, so hours grew longer, inspections were relaxed, and conditions deteriorated. This produced an increasing number of strikes and a deteriorating situation throughout industry, mining and forestry. It also produced a demand that if men were going to be conscripted, then wealth should be conscripted as well, a demand labour shared with the farmers. And like the farmers, labour found that with the Liberals supporting the Conservatives in the war effort, they had no elected politicians to represent their grievances. So they turned to new ones – Labour, Socialist, Communist and even the United Farmers of Ontario.

War accentuated another problem that had been festering for many decades. It greatly strengthened the prohibitionist movement in a number of ways. It was now arguably immoral to convert grain and barley into alcohol when food was needed for the war effort. Liquor sapped the strength of farmers and workers – surely this was unacceptable in wartime. And the war itself had strengthened the voices of the proponents of prohibition – the English, Protestants, and women - and weakened those of immigrants, Catholics and men. There was now clear majority support for total prohibition, and Premier Hearst bowed to the pressure. In March, 1916, the sale and consumption of liquor was banned throughout Ontario. It could still be manufactured for export and for industry, and consumed for medicinal and religious reasons.

War also produced another giant step towards full democracy. All adult men had been enfranchised by 1888, except natives living on reserves, but the decades-long campaign for woman's suffrage had been rejected by all governments. Because of war, women replaced men throughout the economy, in shops, in banks, in the professions, in jobs that were responsible, dangerous, or physically demanding. Time-worn arguments about male superiority or uniqueness could no longer be sustained, and in 1917 Ontario became the fifth province to give women the vote.

Conscription, in which so much political capital had been invested, then proved unnecessary as the conscripts arrived just as the war was ending. The other problems created by war – inflation, shortages, racial tensions, and disgruntled farmers and workers, continued to challenge the over-worked premier. Before he could address them a new batch of problems arose as prices fell, unemployment surged, and hundreds of thousands of battle-hardened soldiers came home to a hero's welcome and no jobs. Euphoria and relief over the victory and the end of the slaughter and pride in a successful wartime effort could not disguise a painful reality – in 1918 the Hearst government was in deep, deep trouble.

Chapter Six
Farmers, Foam and Fergie, 1918 – 1930

On October 20, 1919 the good citizens of Ontario trooped off to vote for a provincial government and yet another referendum on controlling liquor. There were over twice as many electors, because women had the vote for the first time. Confirming prohibition was never in doubt, but little did the voters know that they were about to elect a leaderless party that had not even existed a year earlier. The United Farmers of Ontario or UFO did not expect to win the election. Indeed, they did not even want to. Their goal was to elect enough MPPs to force a Conservative or Liberal government to do more of the things they wanted. Instead, an unlikely group of amateurs was soon wielding power in Queen's Park.

The Conservatives under Hearst entered the campaign expecting to win. After all, in 1914 they had won 84 of 111 seats and the Liberals were hopelessly divided and disorganized. Premier Hearst was a genuine reformer, and he had satisfied the two biggest political demands of the day – prohibition and women's suffrage. For four years the war had dominated all other issues, and he had provided solid support to the war effort. He had continued with the careful and scandal-free administration of the great James P. Whitney. His government had carefully prepared the groundwork for a wide-ranging series of reforms as soon as post-war circumstances allowed. Farmers and workers were grumbling, but they had been grumbling for decades. There was also a recession, inflation, a housing crisis, and few jobs for returning veterans, problems the government was not addressing very well.

Everyone misjudged the depth of the farmer's rage, and the effects it could have in a political system where a plurality of votes won a seat, and where rural votes counted for up to ten times as much as urban votes. Failure to provide "one man, one vote" or "representation by population" was about to bury the two-party system. The farmer's anger had been mounting for decades. In the days before Confederation, they had formed the Clear Grits to demand democracy and pro-agricultural policies. In the 1890s, their discontent had produced an agrarian political revolt which resulted in the election of 19 MPPs from the Patrons of Industry.

Their main grievance was rural depopulation, the steady drift of farmers' sons and daughters to the cities, the prairies and the United States. Machinery meant that fewer hands were needed to work an acre of land. Farmers welcomed that, but somehow failed to see that the inevitable consequence was larger farms, abandoned homesteads, fewer people in the district, an aging rural population, and the closure of small schools and churches. Adding to their concern was their view that the cities their kids were moving to were notorious centres of immorality, slums, immigrants, polluted air and unsafe, unsanitary, boring, repetitive, soul-destroying jobs in dirty factories. Life on the farm, they fervently believed, was morally superior.

For decades these grievances had been brought forcefully to the attention of government, and for decades government had made symbolic, minimal gestures. Instead, it had concentrated its efforts to develop northern Ontario, or produce hydro-electric power for the factories and the spoiled denizens of the cities with their fancy electric gadgets. The price of agricultural products had been falling since the 1880s; the price of agricultural machinery had been artificially raised by perhaps a third by federal tariffs. In the war the government had controlled the price of their products and conscripted their sons. Farmers were no better off than their parents, and they were subsidizing industrialization and the urban standard of living.

The two provincial parties had also agreed to postpone by-elections during the war, so those who disagreed with them had no place to go. Except, that is, to join the local farmer's organization, the UFO. And that is exactly what they did. All across the province farmers were joining the UFO in droves. The number of UFO clubs jumped from 200 in 1916 to 600 in 1918, and tripled again in 1919. J.J. Morrison, President of the UFO, sensed that farmers were going to contest the next provincial election and had a platform drafted. But the movement was grass roots – in dozens of constituencies the members of the UFO decided themselves to nominate candidates. Their headquarters in Toronto was running to catch up, offering some pamphlets, a bit of money, perhaps an outside speaker.

A smaller but equally serious movement was sweeping labour. Their grievances also dated back decades, and emphasized poor working conditions and inadequate pay. They were tired of sops from the government in the form of legislation for better safety and sanitary conditions, legislation that was not supported by inspectors and meaningful enforcement. During the war, wages were held down, prices rose, workers got poorer, and working conditions were ignored. Workers engaged in more and more strikes, with increasing violence on both sides. Since both political parties supported the war effort, workers turned to alternatives, especially the Independent Labour Party or ILP, and the more strident and violent Communist movement.

When the results of the election were announced the province went into shock. The Conservatives had lost 2/3 of their members, leaving a rump of 25, fewer than the Liberals at 27. The UFO had jumped from two seats to 44, 12 short of a majority. The ILP had gone from one to eleven. It took a week to sort out the mess. The UFO decided to form a government. Labour and the UFO were on opposite sides on most issues, but they both hated the Conservatives and Liberals. So Labour decided to support the farmers.

Forming an administration was not easy. The UFO had won the election without a leader. After rejecting four possible contenders, the job was offered with little enthusiasm to Ernest Drury. He was a very successful farmer and businessman, had a university degree, was the son of Mowat's Minister of Agriculture, and had shown political ambition by running for the federal Liberals in 1917. He had proven leadership and management credentials, was a founding member of the UFO, and had drafted the UFO's election platform. Drury was honest, humourless and arrogant, and he could be tough. He did not want the job, but he did not see how the farmers could reject the opportunity to put their ideas into practice. Drury was duly sworn in as Ontario's eighth premier

Drury did not know many of the MLAs, and they did not know each other, so assembling a Cabinet was a challenge. Labour had to be given two ministries. The usual bows had to be made – to the regions, the cities, other interests, the Catholics and a new, powerful and frustrated group, the war veterans. The UFO had 44 candidates for Minister of Agriculture, and none for Attorney General. That job had to be held by a lawyer, and their constitution forbade lawyers from being members. Drury recruited the Liberal MLA William Raney, a fanatical moralist and prohibitionist who became a major liability. None of these compromises came easily to the backbenchers or the UFO secretariat who thought that the UFO had been elected to bring purity to government. Amongst the novice politicians there was, however, quite a wealth of experience in local government. With this Cabinet in place, the UFO prepared to impose its agenda.

Unfortunately, it did not quite have an agenda. What the farmers' movement had was a long list of grievances. It did not, actually, know what to do about most of them. Rural depopulation was a result of industrialization, and could no more be stopped than the oceans' tides. The prices of farm products were determined by international markets, and there was nothing Ontario could do about them. Prohibition was already in effect, and tariffs were a federal responsibility. Labour and the farmers were on opposite sides of many issues. The farmers wanted cheaper industrial goods and a better price for their products; labour wanted higher wages and cheaper food.

In the absence of its own program, the UFO brought in the legislation the previous government had prepared, much of it borrowed from the more progressive western provinces. That included minimum wage for women, mothers' allowances, improvements to workman's compensation, better health services, pensions for civil servants, increased funding for education, and particularly improved protection for children. Farmers had complained for years about declining morality, and launched a campaign of "moral uplift", another lost cause. Farmers had long thought that northern Ontario received too much attention, and the UFO shut down the northern development programs. This was successful to the point that demand arose in the north to create a separate province! The government refused to deal with the French language issue, and in the next election the French Catholic clergy urged its defeat.

The UFOs greatest achievement came with Ontario Hydro. Chairman Adam Beck was extremely ambitious, and was managing a rapidly expanding and extremely powerful empire with little supervision from the government. He was actively involved in creating new demand, in advertising the wonders of new electric appliances and applications, in promoting rural electrification, in buying out private hydro companies, and in knitting them into a bigger and better network. One of his plans was to create a system of electric trains connecting the major cities. The cost was enormous, and they would duplicate the existing system of railways and compete with the highways the province was building. Drury decided that his government would not repeat the mistakes of previous ones which had overbuilt railways. He shut the project down, and Ontario was saved a potentially catastrophic investment in electric railways.

Drury also wondered why power plants like the Chippawa one at Niagara cost six times the original estimate. He called for studies which revealed that every Ontario Hydro project had cost far more than the estimates. He asked to see the books. Beck stalled and then provided insufficient information. Drury asked again, and demanded better accounting. Beck withdrew Hydro advertising from newspapers that took the government's side in the dispute, and made speeches condemning government policy. That called into question the degree of freedom a publicly-owned utility could and should have. Drury won the battle, and the free-wheeling ways of Hydro's chairman were brought under control.

On other matters the farmers seemed adrift, confused and divided. Their goal of establishing a group government similar to a large municipality foundered on the principle of party politics which had dominated the province for generations. They promised economy in government, and increased spending by 200%. Frustrated with their failure to enforce prohibition, they created a special police force. Its heavy-handed tactics undermined respect for the law. They failed to implement their democratic agenda of recall, initiative, and the transferable ballot, and opposed redistribution. Then, in spite of their overwhelming farm base, they spent most of the rapidly increasing highways budget on provincial instead of rural roads.

Such policies brought them into repeated conflict with the UFO and with their own backbenchers and supporters. But Drury's arrogance and the self-satisfaction of moral superiority blinded him to the need to listen and to compromise. The rejuvenated Conservatives under Howard Ferguson ripped the government apart in the Assembly, forced it to abandon policies, and exploited the divisions between farmer and worker and between the government and its supporters. When the government launched a major investigation into Ferguson's handling of the Lands and Forests portfolio in the previous administration, his brilliant defence made him the undisputed leader of the opposition. Drury was forced to call an election for June 25, 1923.

Howard Ferguson created a formidable political machine which won 75 of 111 seats, reducing the UFO to 17, the Liberals to 14 and Labour to four. He won a majority of the popular vote, and would win over 50% in the elections of 1926 and 1929. Ferguson, or "Foxie Fergie", was a consummate politician, one of the best in Ontario's history. Coming from the town of Kemptville south of Ottawa, he understood farmers, businesspeople, ordinary folk, Protestants and Catholic, and the English-Scots-Irish-French mix of the population. In politics he came to understand other regions, the cities and big business. He talked easily to anyone, listened carefully to everyone, and those people believed that he understood them. He was big, happy, and outgoing, but he was tough and decisive, had a superb memory, and was a great organizer and administrator.

Throughout his career Ferguson grew intellectually and emotionally. He put behind him his past as a small-town Orange militant, and made Catholics a bastion of Conservative strength. He thought that one of the many mistakes the UFO had made was to introduce too much legislation, so he introduced very little. He thought there had been too much politics, so he cut back on the sittings of the Assembly and on its activities. He appointed good ministers and let them get on with the work of administering their departments, but he kept himself independently informed of their work and could easily rescue them if they got into difficulties.

Ferguson handled patronage and scandals carefully, quietly and well. When a minister was accused of wrongdoing; Ferguson dismissed him, and for the most part his administration avoided scandal. He had excellent relations with his federal Conservative cousins, with the press, and with other premiers, especially his Liberal counterpart across the Ottawa River. Within that political framework, his government undertook a massive road-building program, substantial support for northern development and education, and contributed directly to the economic boom that swept the province in the late 1920s.

The most important issue that Ferguson had to deal with was prohibition, and it dominated the election of 1926 and, to a lesser extent, that of 1929. Part of the problem was that prohibition was simply impossible - government could not stop people from drinking alcohol and the real questions were when, where, and how alcohol would be consumed. The problem was that a large portion of the population simply would not accept that basic fact. They clung with religious fervour to the belief that government could eliminate totally and forever the consumption of alcohol, if only it tried just a little harder.

Ferguson had to find a path between these two truisms, knowing that many Conservatives were prohibitionists. Another consideration for him was the fact that the government was spending substantial resources on a failed program – up to half the law enforcement budget in some areas – and losing significant revenues it could have been collecting from liquor taxes. That was extremely important to the government because it was running a deficit in a period of economic prosperity.

The problems created by prohibition were everywhere in evidence. It was legal to produce alcohol for export, and legally exported alcohol was easily smuggled back into the province. It was legal for farmers to make their own beer and wine, and that exposed the hypocrisy of the farmers' prohibitionist crusade. As always the rich found ways to fill their needs. For centuries alcohol has been used as medicine. Ontario never banned that use, and the thirsty quickly exploited the loophole. One doctor issued 6,000 prescriptions in a month, another wrote close to 500 in a single day, a provincial total of 800,000 in 1923. Prohibition was turning drinkers into criminals, along with anyone who served or protected them – doctors, druggists taxi drivers, hotel owners, restaurant workers, bartenders, and worst of all, the politicians, the police and the courts. In addition, thousands of people made their own liquor illegally, sometimes with devastating effects on health. Inspectors who were bribed to turn a blind eye to drinking in hotels also ignored unsanitary conditions.

The solution was not to plug the leaks in the system, as governments had tried to do for half a century, but rather to end the system itself. In the 1923 election Ferguson's approach was to let his candidates whisper that a conservative government would be sympathetic to a loosening of the regulations. His first major effort to end prohibition was to make it legal to sell "non-intoxicating" beer with only 2.5% alcohol content. It was dubbed "Fergie's Foam", and some experiments proved that a normal male could not consume enough of it to become intoxicated. Devout prohibitionists were outraged, but most people drank beer for the taste or to socialize, not to get drunk, and they were satisfied with the product. Beer with alcohol content was back on the market.

Ferguson knew that prohibition could not be abolished, but had to be replaced with a reasonable alternative. His solution was to implement a system of extremely limited access to alcohol which could be made to work, and which would prevent the abuses that had led to prohibition in the first place. His plan was to make liquor available, but under extremely stringent rules, with each constituency to decide whether it was wet or dry. In the constituencies that voted wet, men over 21 could have a beer in a pub, and men and women could drink at home or in a hotel room. No one could drink in a restaurant or bar. Men could get a licence to buy alcohol, but only at a government-run store, which kept a record of their purchases and enforced limits on the amount they bought. No liquor advertising was allowed.

The 1926 election was fought on this issue – maintain the existing regime or replace it with strict government control. Ferguson's top Cabinet Minister and many party supporters resigned. The Protestant churches rose up in protest. Much of the press was opposed. Ferguson, however, had read the public mood correctly. He had also arranged a redistribution of seats. It partially corrected the exaggerated strength of rural votes, and that reduced the number of dry constituencies from 69 to 59. The Conservatives took an unprecedented 56% of the popular vote and 74 seats, to 14 for the Liberals and 24 divided between seven other parties. The Liquor Control Board of Ontario (LCBO) was established, with emphasis on the word "control". Sales boomed, and the province balanced its budget for the first time in years. Ferguson had ended prohibition. From then on, the challenge for politicians would be to modify the strict regulations he had to impose to get rid of the impossible policy, a process that continues to this day.

Freedom to drink, such as it was, fitted perfectly into the mood of the late 1920s. Car ownership was booming, giving parents access to cottages and to more distant retreats, and giving youths an escape from over-protective parents. For the first time Ontarians began to discover their province – "Yours to Discover" is still emblazoned on their licence plates. Movies were all the rage, along with new, exciting and somewhat sexy dances. Relaxed mores were reflected in the shorter length of women's skirts and the fact that they could be seen smoking in public. Farm prices had improved taking the bitterness out of the UFO's failures, and mining was booming, adding to the frenzy on the Toronto Stock Exchange. Prosperity and optimism allowed Ferguson to turn to other unfinished business and to new challenges.

Another ghost that Ferguson laid to rest was one partially of his own making, namely Regulation 17. That rule, adopted in 1912, was designed to ensure that Franco-Ontarian students emerged from school capable of functioning in an English-speaking province. Franco-Ontarians believed they had a "right" to use French in their schools, but they lost that battle in a series of court decisions. By the mid 1920s most of them had accepted that defeat. Equally important, by the mid-1920s they had accepted that to function and prosper in Ontario, their children had to speak some

English. They had, in effect, accepted the purpose of Regulation 17.

With the French no longer insisting on "rights" that were not in the Constitution, and with their schools now producing students who spoke some English, Ferguson moved to modify the regulations that were designed to force English upon them. The government acknowledged the fact of French-language schools, and accepted French language instruction up to the end of primary school. Taxes paid by French Canadians that had previously been diverted to the public schools were now directed to the French ones. That helped address their financial problems and hence improve the quality of the teachers and of their education. The University of Ottawa's French normal school was recognized. The Orange Lodge protested such "concessions", but that voice was weakened by the fact that Ferguson was still an Orangeman.

While these issues were playing out, an old problem came back to haunt Ontario politics, namely, the efforts of the federal government to intrude into provincial areas of responsibility. The issue was hydro-electric power. Ontario's economy was booming, and a power shortage was looming. Developing the Ottawa River was the best option. It was a navigational stream, and by the constitution, Ottawa was responsible for navigation. Rapids on the river also created a potential for hydro-electric power, a provincial responsibility. Logically, the solution was for one or both governments to build a dam, share the costs, divert some of the water into the canal which the federal government would pay for, and divert some of the water into a power plant, which the province would pay for. Unfortunately, the politicians and mandarins in Ottawa had decided that federal control over canals could be leveraged into control over the development of hydro-electric power.

No Ontario government could accept such a proposition, because that could give Ottawa control of the hydro-electric power of any navigable river in the province. Interpreted broadly, as Ottawa was prone to do, that could give the federal government control over much of Ontario's economy. This was a new and perplexing development, as Ottawa had never questioned Ontario's control of power plants at Niagara.

Ferguson ally in this war was Quebec Premier Alexandre Taschereau, who was even more concerned with Ottawa's penchant for interfering in provincial jurisdiction. Regulation 17 was an obstacle to cooperation, however, because it was seen in Quebec as an attempt by bigoted Englishmen to deny language rights to French Canadian Ontarians that English Canadians enjoyed in Quebec. Taschereau raised Regulation 17 with Ferguson, and that may have been an important factor in Ferguson's decision to recognize French language education. Over-riding all these issues, however, was the fact that the two governments were in complete agreement on rejecting Ottawa's attempt to take control of the Ottawa River. After many complicated negotiations, an agreement emerged whereby Quebec companies would sell a significant quantity of power to Ontario over thirty years. Ontario's needs had been met. Ferguson had stood up to Ottawa, and Ottawa had obtained nothing except ill-will.

Hydro was the biggest, but not the only, irritant in federal-provincial relations. Ottawa attempted once more to regulate insurance companies. The Ontario Supreme Court sided with Ontario, but Ottawa refused to recognize that decision. The issue was appealed to the Judicial Committee of the Privy Council (JCPC), which decided for Ontario. The JCPC had also sided with Ontario on the question of which level of government had responsibility for industrial disputes, but Ottawa ignored that decision. Ottawa also tried to make loan and trust companies obtain federal licences after Ontario alone had been regulating them for decades.

These disputes were to have a very serious long-term effect on Canada. As in the 1880s, Ontario saw the JCPC in London as essential for defending provincial jurisdiction from federal encroachment. In the 1920s, Ottawa wanted to patriate the constitution. Ontario was opposed because then a federally-appointed Supreme Court would replace the JCPC as the supreme arbiter of federal-provincial disputes, and presumably be more favourable to the federal government. Provincial opposition would postpone the patriation of the constitution for half a century, and ultimately make amending the constitution extremely difficult. In 1931 Ontario obtained British agreement that sections of the BNA Act that affected provinces could not be amended without provincial agreement. It was the logical conclusion of all the federal-provincial disputes the JCPC had heard over the previous half century, and it was the greatest victory ever for provincial rights in Canada.

Ferguson was treated as a hero for his victory in these battles. The election of October 30, 1929, was another overwhelming rout, with a record 57% of the popular vote producing 92 seats compared to 13 for the Liberals, and seven for the four other parties. Ferguson then threw his support solidly behind the federal Conservatives in the national election of 1930. He had said that he wanted to retire from Ontario politics around the age of 60, and to leave time for a successor to become established. A grateful federal government made him High Commissioner to London. Before going he nominated George Henry to replace him, and the caucus agreed. The timing was not fortuitous for Henry – Ontario was just entering the worst economic crisis of its history.

Chapter Seven
The Depression and Mitch Hepburn, 1930 – 1942

Before Ferguson left for London, the Great Depression of the 1930s had begun. It was a national and global catastrophe, and it hit Ontario with devastating effect. The cycle of economic "boom and bust" had gone on for generations, with periods of great economic activity and increasing prosperity followed by periods of stagnation, falling income, and poverty for many. There had been recessions in the 1860s, the 1870s, and before and after World War I, each one followed by good times.

The recession that began in 1929 with the collapse of the New York stock market quickly became much worse than previous ones. Countries sought to protect domestic industry by raising tariffs to exclude foreign goods. The policy failed. Exports from all countries declined, the relative cost of goods increased, and factories laid off workers. Banks called in their loans and made it difficult for companies or people to borrow. Investment almost ceased, and with it the jobs and the demand for goods that investment created. There was an immediate drop in the amount of money in circulation. People became more frugal, so the demand for goods declined even more. Factories laid off even more workers in a downward spiral of decreasing economic activity and consumption, rising unemployment, and increasing poverty, confusion and misery.

Though Ontario was less severely affected than any other province, industrial production fell by half, the construction industry declined by 65%, farm prices declined 50%, lumber production fell 70%, automobile production fell by 80%, and the stock market fell by 80%. By 1933, the worst year, 500,000 people were on welfare.

The problems of welfare, unemployment, and of rural people flooding into the towns and cities overwhelmed municipal governments. Declining property taxes and fixed payments on previous debts left municipalities incapable of coping with the rising demand for welfare. Soon the provincial government had to take over welfare and relief from the municipalities, with Queen's Park paying half and Ottawa paying half. The Conservative provincial government was not prepared to deal with the Depression financially, politically, or ideologically. When revenue fell, Premier Henry cut expenditures and increased taxes. The spending cuts added to unemployment, and the unemployed spent less, further reducing the demand for goods and services. The tax increases took money out of people's pockets, which reduced demand even more.

Premier George Henry was an experienced politician, Ferguson's acknowledged second-in-command. He was a successful farmer and businessman, equally at home at a county fair or on Bay Street. He was hard-working, blunt, cold, and overly cautious. Like Canadian politicians at all levels, he had no idea of how to deal with the Depression. And like too many of them, he believed there actually were many unfilled jobs available, and that the unemployed simply were not trying hard enough to find work. His unsuitability to lead a province in economic crisis was revealed when accusations were made that his government was doing business with a company in which he owned $25,000 in stock. He seemed to have forgotten that he owned the stock - the unemployed probably thought that he had forgotten about them too.

The government created massive make-work projects, including the completion of the railway to Moosonee on James Bay and the Trans-Canada Highway (Highway 17). At one time 40,000 men were working on highways, airports and other public works. Conditions were terrible, and the work camps radicalized the men, making them hard-line unionists when they did get jobs, and potential supporters of the Communist Party. Welfare was distributed in the most parsimonious way possible. Recipients could not own cars, buy liquor or cosmetics, or receive welfare if they obtained money from any other source. Welfare often came in the form of vouchers to buy specific types of goods in stores. If repairs had to be made, the home owner had to go to the municipal office and obtain a special voucher for that particular job. Thus humiliation was heaped on misery.

While many people suffered, many others gained from the crisis. The cost of living fell 20%, so those on salaries or fixed incomes from bonds became richer. Tariffs protected the jobs of many workers, and northern Ontario experienced another mining boom. Those who benefited opposed reforms that would help the poor. The paradox of the few growing richer while the many suffered added to the bitterness of the times, and led to ugly demonstrations, violent strikes, and growing radicalism. To make matters worse, the federal and provincial governments played pass-the-buck, each arguing that unemployment was the responsibility of the other level of government.

As the Henry government floundered in helpless confusion, a new messiah emerged to lead the Liberals out of three decades in the political wilderness. Mitchell Hepburn, or "Mitch", was the most erratic premier the province would ever know. He was impulsive, quick-tempered, emotional, stubborn, irresponsible, irreverent, unpredictable, unstable, and uncontrollable. He dropped out of high school to avoid being expelled, and maturing seemed to involve the discovery of liquor and women, which he enjoyed indiscreetly and to excess. He was also charming, bright, loyal, and capable of taking principled stands, a great public speaker, and an extremely popular "populist" politician. As someone said, he was a sinner, but he was not a bad man.

Mitch won a seat for the federal Liberals in 1926. When the King government went down to defeat in 1930, he survived with an increased vote. By then the provincial Liberals were looking for a leader amongst an unimpressive group of contenders, and in desperation they turned to Mitch. Hepburn immediately went to work re-building the party. He toured the province extensively, and a clear pattern emerged. He would speak to a number of small gatherings – short, clear speeches, lambasting the government and setting out the areas where the

Liberals would do things better. He would meet the local Liberal organizers, and infuse them with a sense of confidence. He would shake hands along main street, easily making friends and gathering support. Then he and his colleagues would retire to a hotel room and party till the wee hours. The next day he would sleep in the car until they arrived in the next town, and then do it all over again.

Hepburn assembled an excellent slate of candidates and a strong organization to support them. His election platform identified major areas of government policy for criticism, with broad hints about what his government would do differently. He deliberately moved the party to the left, cultivating Labour, the remnants of the UFO and the Progressives. He made strategic vote-sharing arrangements with those parties, and he kept on good terms with the federal Liberals, now also in opposition. And he campaigned long and hard in the 1934 election.

Once more the control of liquor was a major issue. Premier Henry realized that the strict rules had to be eased. As an act of political desperation he introduced legislation allowing the sale of beer and wine in hotels, taverns and restaurants. The drys were disgusted, and the wets had a choice of voting for a prohibitionist who violated his principles or a man who consumed alcohol publicly and excessively. On other issues like solving the Depression or support for Catholic schools, Hepburn exhibited a willingness to question traditional policies and to provide leadership in finding solutions.

When the results came in on June 19, 1934, Ontario had changed ruling parties for only the fifth time in its history. The Liberals were now in power with 65 out of 90 seats, based on a majority of the popular vote and strength in every part of the province. The Conservatives had fallen to 17 and other parties shared eight. One seat went to the new Cooperative Commonwealth Federation, a party that emerged on the prairies during the Depression as a socialist party proposing a vastly expanded role for government in the economy, the nationalization of key industries and businesses, increased government spending, easier credit to stimulate the economy in times of recession, and increased taxes on the wealthy to pay for substantially improved health and welfare systems. It would be a factor in Ontario politics from then on.

Mitch appointed a good, strong, balanced Cabinet, keeping the key position of Treasurer for himself. The new government launched a flood of reforms to help address the Depression and bring hope back into people's lives. They improved the administration of welfare, government departments, industrial disputes and health, and introduced a minimum wage for men and pensions for the blind. They cancelled construction contracts, cut the size of the civil service by 10%, and ended the attempts to develop agricultural colonies in the north. The government auctioned off ministers' limousines, sold the Lieutenant Governor's mansion and closed Ontario House in London. These measures sent a message – Hepburn's cabinet ministers would drive their own cars, just like any other car owner. The symbolism was enormous – poor farmers were being forced to park their trucks and revert to using horse and wagon. With the money saved by all these measures, the government increased grants to the municipalities.

One of the first problems Hepburn tackled was the unfairness of government policy towards Catholic schools. By law, Catholics could designate their property taxes for separate schools, but since the 1850s, the Protestants who ran the local governments had made that very difficult. Company taxes, for example, were often applied entirely to the public schools, even if some of the shareholders were Catholic. As a result public schools had far more revenue than Catholic ones, allowing Protestant extremists to gloat about lower standards in Catholic schools. Hepburn introduced legislation to force companies to identify which school the shareholders wanted their tax to go to. Protestants complained, and Cabinet debated the issue for hours.

Near dawn on the third day of the Assembly debate, Hepburn delivered an emotional speech, saying it was time to treat the Catholic minority fairly. The legislation failed to pass, but Catholics knew that a premier had finally stood up for them, and many Protestants realized that the system was grossly unfair. Hepburn then quietly increased the government's grants to separate schools, and solved administratively a problem that could not be solved politically. It was perhaps his finest battle.

Other battles were not as principled. One of the biggest problems he inherited was power supply. His government was stuck with the 30-year contracts Premier Ferguson had negotiated with the Quebec companies. At the time, it was an excellent deal, but the Depression reduced Ontario Hydro's sales by 50% while it still had to pay for the full amount contracted. By 1934 Ontario Hydro was in serious financial trouble, and the Hepburn government threatened to cancel the contracts. The struggle grew to gigantic proportions, with the private sector and media backing the companies, the Quebec government trying to protect its companies, Ontario threatening to stop buying any power from Quebec, and Ottawa threatening to intervene.

The banks refused to buy Ontario government bonds. Hepburn accused them of trying to dictate policy and offered bonds directly to the public. The bonds were immediately bought up, so the banks backed off. The fight went on for years, the final outcome being that Ontario lost the court battle to repudiate the contracts, but the companies agreed to re-negotiate the terms. Hydro rates were reduced by 17%, and Hepburn claimed that he had saved $6,000,000 a year, the equivalent of 10% of the provincial budget. Mitch was rapidly gaining a reputation as the man who could stand up to Ottawa, the banks, and big business, all of which were disliked and distrusted by the poor and the unemployed, the "little people" whom Mitch represented.

Another area of violent political battle, and another one where Mitch seemed to change sides was labour. In the early 1930s he wooed Labour, and his first administration made a number of genuine improvements in workers' conditions. But as the economy recovered, the number on welfare did not fall proportionately. Farmers complained that they could not hire workers. In Welland, a number of men on a make-work project went on strike for higher wages. Mitch was infuriated with what he saw as ingratitude and greed. As demand grew for manufactured goods, the unions started going on strike for higher wages. Hepburn threw one-third the cost of welfare back on the municipalities, partly to force them to be tougher with welfare recipients who could find work but, in his opinion, choose not to.

The problem came to a head with a strike at the General Motors plant at Oshawa. The workers wanted better wages and conditions, which the company was willing to negotiate. They also wanted recognition of their union as part of the Congress of Industrial Organization or CIO, a powerful, militant, Communist-infiltrated American union that had won major battles with the big American companies. Hepburn had no intention of allowing a tough American union to expand in Canada, especially one with Communist connections. He feared, in particular, for what such a union might do in the mining sector, and he was determined to stop its progress at Oshawa. His concerns were exaggerated, but they were shared by business, the press, the Conservative opposition, part of the federal government, and a wide sector of the public.

Mitch was not one to be pushed around by unions. He informed Ottawa that the union was engaged in a sit-down strike, and asked for RCMP help. Sit down strikes were illegal, and Ottawa sent 100 constables. But the union was actually engaged in legal picketing, not a sit-down strike. When Ottawa learned that, it ordered the RCMP to withdraw. Mitch asked for more constables, and PM Mackenzie King refused. Mitch felt betrayed, and had the Ontario Provincial Police recruit 200 volunteers, soon to be knows as Hepburn's Hussars or the Sons of Mitches. Hepburn had over-reacted - the special police were not needed.

The GM strike actually produced a six-sided showdown. The provincial government split on the issue, and two of the best ministers resigned. The federal government was also divided, but King's views on withholding support from Hepburn prevailed. There was yet another bitter federal-provincial fight, which left Ottawa thinking that Hepburn had misled them, and Hepburn feeling betrayed by Ottawa's reluctance to help. There was the strike itself. And then there was the showdown between Ontario and the CIO. In fact the company and the workers wanted a solution, and they negotiated it. The workers got better conditions and their union was recognized, but not as the CIO. In that sense it was a victory for Hepburn. The deal was signed in his office, and the name of the CIO was not on it. But Mitch had made enemies, and he travelled with a revolver and had 24 hour police protection on his house.

By 1937 Mitch and King hated each other with a passion so great that their personal animosity had become a major factor in Ontario and national politics. Mitch had strongly supported the federal Liberals in their successful 1935 campaign. But when he recommended a certain Cabinet appointment, King not only ignored him but selected as Finance Minister a fiscal conservative who would reject Hepburn's most urgent requests. Hepburn wanted federal action on lowering tariffs, having the Bank of Canada introduce easier credit and lower interest rates, and federal acceptance of more responsibility for welfare and unemployment. King rejected every request and reduced further the federal share of municipal welfare costs. In 1937 Hepburn severed the links between the provincial and federal parties, informing the Ottawa Liberals that they were neither needed nor wanted in the upcoming provincial election.

In the election of October 6, 1937, Hepburn took nothing for granted, campaigning hard for seven weeks, making effective use of radio and advertising, and emphasizing his record and the weaknesses of the opposition. The record included traditional policies like economies in government, a balanced budget, help for municipalities, increased pensions, road-building, and standing up to Ottawa, the banks and the big companies. He did not mention his efforts to treat Catholic schools fairly, but the Conservatives made it an issue. He also managed to hide the contradictions in his energy policy until after the election. It all worked, the Liberals gaining 51 % of the popular vote, but losing six seats, the Conservatives gaining these six with 41% of the vote. The new CCF lost the one seat it had won in 1934.

When the Depression struck, Canadian politicians had no idea how to cope with it, and had carried on with traditional policies. Hepburn did the same, but he was also one of a few who were willing to question, modify and perhaps discard some of those traditional policies. In one of his first speeches he said that the underlying problem was reduced demand or consumption, which could be solved by having the federal government make credit available, in other words, print money to pay for make-work projects and relief. There had, in fact, been a serious curtailment of credit and resulting deflation after the depression began. Immediately after his election in 1934 Hepburn had asked Prime Minister Bennett to call a federal-provincial conference to discuss monetary reform, but Bennett refused.

In 1935 Hepburn thought the new Canadian Prime Minister, Mackenzie King, would be more receptive. King, however, refused to even study the suitability of existing monetary policies, and vetoed every measure the new Social Credit government in Alberta introduced to increase the money supply. Oddly, though, when World War II broke out, the federal government did create credit to help pay for it, and Ottawa has used credit expansion ever since to stimulate the economy in times of recession. Hepburn was right to challenge existing economic theory, to advocate change, and he was right in the solution he proposed, namely, easier credit during recession. King's refusal to even consider change infuriated the provincial Premier.

King's answer to the Depression was, instead, to appoint a Royal Commission to study the constitutional aspects of dealing with it. To him, the areas that needed more government spending – welfare, unemployment and public works – were all provincial, but the federal government had the taxing power to address them. There were three possible solutions – transfer some provincial responsibilities to Ottawa, transfer some of Ottawa's taxing power to the provinces, or implement some combination of the two. The battle lines were drawn early on: the federal government and the poorest provinces wanted to transfer provincial responsibilities to Ottawa; the richer prov-

History of Ontario

inces and Quebec wanted to transfer federal taxation power to the provinces. The mandate of the Rowell-Sirois commission was to investigate these constitutional issues. Hepburn saw the Commission as an attempt by Ottawa to use the Depression to strengthen federal power at the expense of the provinces. He had a very sound case, one that Quebec, BC and Alberta supported, the four representing an overwhelming majority of Canadians.

Tactically, though, Hepburn's presentation before the Royal Commission was a disaster. He questioned its usefulness, defended provincial jurisdiction, and said that an increase in federal power could lead to dictatorship. His position appeared to be that Canada's richest and most populous province had no moral or national obligation to help the poorer provinces. His presentation and conduct at the meetings and the receptions shocked the other delegates as well as the media. As was too often the case with Hepburn, questions arose as to whether his ill health, excessive drinking, late night carousing and hatred of King were not affecting his judgement and the conduct of government business. In a sense it did not matter – the Commission proceeded to study federalism while the Depression drifted on for another three years.

The outbreak of World War II in September, 1939, brought the Depression to a speedy end as the federal government issued hundreds of millions of dollars worth of credit for contracts for military equipment, recruiting soldiers, and building camps. That launched an industrial and a construction boom which produced a secondary boom in forestry and mining, and people spent more on food so the price of agricultural products rose. By 1940 labour shortages were beginning to appear.

Ontario threw itself solidly into the wartime effort, as it had in World War I. The Hepburn government immediately put itself on a wartime footing, sending guards to the hydro facilities, giving Ontario Hydro the authority to ration power, arresting potential enemy sympathisers, and expressing a willingness to cooperate with the federal government. However, in the opinion of Hepburn and many other Ontarians, Ottawa did not prosecute the war with sufficient vigour.

The wartime effort was debated in the Assembly in January, 1940, and to the amazement of the members, Hepburn introduced a motion criticizing Ottawa's commitment to the war effort. It was a direct challenge to federal authority in wartime, a huge political mistake. The motion passed 44-10, with support from the Conservatives but with 20 Liberals either absent or voting against it. A federal election was due in 1940, and King used the challenge to call it immediately, trouncing the Conservative opposition and thoroughly weakening Hepburn's political standing.

By late 1940, however, the federal government was doing almost all it could, and the war effort was beginning to strain Ottawa's capacity to raise money by taxation, borrowing and creating credit. King could have called a federal-provincial conference on financing the war, and would probably have obtained provincial agreement to the surrender of provincial taxes for the duration of the war. That had been done in World War I without difficulty. Instead, King called a conference for January 1941 to consider the recommendations of the Rowell-Sirois Report for dealing with a Depression that had started eleven years earlier and ended in 1939. To no one's surprise, the Royal Commission had recommended a transfer of provincial jurisdiction and some provincial taxing power to Ottawa so that Canada could better cope with future recessions.

Once more, Hepburn was furious. He saw the Report and the Conference as an attempt by Ottawa to use wartime nationalism and patriotic support for the central government as a lever to effect a permanent change in the constitutional balance between the two levels of government. Once more his position was strategically sound, and he had the support of three other provinces. But once more his tactics and presentation were inexcusably inept. He pointed out quite correctly that the British Government would not appreciate having to deal with amending the BNA Act when it was facing immediate defeat at the hands of the German air force. But he went too far, compared King's machinations to those of Hitler, and thoroughly discredited his own case. Hepburn and the premiers of Quebec, Alberta and BC prevented Mackenzie King from changing the constitution; but they were seen as obstructing the wartime effort.

Everyone understood that Ottawa needed more financial powers to fight the war and that if the provinces did not cooperate, Ottawa would introduce double taxation. The provinces, including Ontario, therefore approved Ottawa's temporary takeover of provincial taxing rights for the duration of the war. Much of Ottawa's wartime spending was done, in fact, in Ontario, touching off a boom in industry, mining, forestry, farming, and the creation of new industries like the petrochemical works at Sarnia and the aircraft factories near Toronto. And hundreds of thousands of Ontarians went off to war just as their parents had done just two decades earlier.

Chapter Eight
The beginning of the Conservative Dynasty, 1942 – 1961

Wartime produced the sixth change of governing party in the province's history. One condition for change is when a governing party runs out of energy, ideas, youth, initiative, good leadership and the capacity to respond to change. Hepburn's life style and the burdens of office had definitely worn him down, and in 1942 he resigned as premier. On his recommendation the lieutenant governor appointed Gordon Conant as premier. The party, however, did not approve, and they selected Harry Nixon instead. Nixon had the necessary experience, but he inherited a divided party, a weakened government, and a bare financial cupboard. The federal government was another liability because it had imposed prohibition nation-wide which reduced Ontario's tax revenues.

The other condition for changing regimes is for the opposition to find good leadership and become a viable alternate in terms of policies and capable potential ministers. That began to happen in 1939 when the Tories selected George Drew, a lawyer, publicist and mayor of Guelph. Drew was a tall, handsome and dashing gentleman, with a distinguished war record. He was smart, tough, well-educated, and self-confident to the point of arrogance. His English-Protestant background was reflected in his pro-British view and a distrust of Catholics and the French. He did not like mixing with the people, and regarded meeting any group as a formal event. But he was Mitch's equal in the Assembly and on the campaign trail, which meant that he was more than the equal of Conant or Nixon.

Drew put together another necessary ingredient for victory – an attractive platform. It was called the Twenty Two Points, and was allegedly drafted on the back of an envelope. It called for improvements to health, welfare, pensions, housing and education especially technical education, for better management and tax regimes for lands, mines, forests, and prisons, for new agricultural marketing boards, reforms to the liquor control regime, provincial payment of half the costs of education, the creation of jobs for veterans, a massive road-building program, and collective bargaining for labour.

Nixon did not prepare well for the election that he called for August 4, 1943. His party was hopelessly divided, and their star candidate, Hepburn, did not campaign. The CCF was growing quickly but was seen by many as too radical. The Conservatives were rejuvenated, united, well-organized, and had strong finances. When the results of the election came in, the Conservatives had the largest vote share at 36% and the largest number of seats at 38, well short of a majority. The Liberals were reduced to 15 and would spend the next four decades in the political wilderness defending old causes and small regions. The CCF had surged to 34 seats based on 32% of the vote, becoming the official Opposition for the first time. After the results were announced, George Drew was sworn in as the 14th premier on August 17.

While the political situation was sorting itself out, Ontario was carrying more than its share of Canada's wartime effort. Over 350,000 men and women were in uniform. Industries were running at full capacity, and indeed, Ontario was one of the powerhouses of the entire Allied effort, supplying much war materiel to Britain and even to the Soviet Union. To support these industries, mining, lumbering and agriculture were in top gear, and new industries had arisen to produce aircraft and artificial rubber. With so many men in the forces, women became a significant portion of the workforce. Unlike the period after World War I, this time many of them remained in the workforce, gradually gaining greater equality with men.

Within the limits of wartime financing, Drew began to implement his Twenty Two Points. One of the most important changes was creating a Department of Planning to move the government to a higher level of organization for the post-war period, and to coordinate issues that involved several departments such as conservation, water management, flood control, or town planning.

Drew soon ran into the obstacle that Mitch had predicted. Mitch believed that the Mackenzie King government was going to use the wartime emergency to try to make a fundamental shift in the constitution, and to permanently take over many provincial responsibilities. To fight the war Ottawa had to control the economy and have the finances to pay for the effort, but the war and the financial agreements were temporary. By 1944 it was becoming clear that Ottawa did, indeed, intend to keep the increased taxing power, and to use it for welfare, a clear provincial responsibility.

On one aspect of welfare there was broad agreement, namely, that Ottawa should take over unemployment and introduce a single system from coast to coast. That consensus had developed during the Depression, partly because the unemployed had moved from province to province, and it was the major recommendation of the Rowell-Sirois report. By 1945 even Ontario was willing to accept that constitutional amendment.

But in 1944 Ottawa announced, without consulting the provinces, a program of family welfare, or baby bonuses, with an equal, federal payment for every child in the country. Drew was infuriated, and immediately denounced the program as an invasion of provincial jurisdiction, and as transferring money from (English Protestant) Ontario to (French Catholic) Quebec. That was true, but it sounded like racism and bigotry. Drew was reflecting two deep feelings in Ontario, namely, concern that Catholic French Canadians had a higher birth rate than Protestants, and that they had not supported the war effort as enthusiastically as had English Canadians. Hepburn, who was once more Liberal leader, was equally outraged by the federal invasion of provincial jurisdiction, but condemned Drew's other arguments as racist.

At that time, Ontario was contributing 50% of all federal taxes, which meant that half of the $200,000,000 federal budget for the new program would come from Ontario taxpayers. Drew argued that if Ontario collected that sum, it would spend it in different ways, including what he saw as the better policies in his Twenty Two Point program. It was also clear to Drew that Mackenzie King and the federal Liberals would be using Ontario's money to reinforce their electoral support in Quebec. Ottawa, however, was not interested in Drew's opinions. It used its wartime emergency powers to pass the legislation creating the family allowance, causing some puzzlement as to how supporting babies helped win the war.

As the war was coming to an end, the two opposition parties decided to defeat the minority Conservative government in March, 1945. The Conservatives, however, were ready for an election, with a good record, excellent candidates, a full war chest, and modern advertising. The Liberals were in poor shape, having had four leaders in three years – Hepburn, Conant, Nixon and Hepburn again. The CCF's promises of state intervention allowed the Conservatives to paint the election as a battle between socialism and free enterprise. On June 4, 1945, the Conservatives swept 66 seats on 45% of the vote, the CCF dropped from 34 to 8 seats on 22% of the vote, and the Liberals became the opposition again with 11 seats and 30% of the vote. It would be three decades before either party could seriously challenge the Conservatives.

The boom that began in 1940 carried on into the post-war era, actually continuing until the recession of 1958. The population exploded from 4.6 million in 1941 to 6.2 million two decades later. It evolved again, with the British component shrinking from 66% to 50%. The rural population fell below 10%, while urbanization continued apace – 60% of Ontarians lived in cities with over 30,000 people. In the war Ontario had produced hundreds of thousands of vehicles, and that level of production continued with cars, trucks, tractors and all manner of machinery. Canada emerged from the war with one of the biggest aircraft industries in the world. By 1945 the giant petro-chemical factory at Sarnia was well established, switching from artificial rubber to plastics and nylon.

Unlike 1918, returning veterans were quickly absorbed into the booming economy. The Depression and war-time rationing had ensured that since 1929, millions of Canadians had spent very little on cars, appliances, clothing, new housing or even repairs to old houses. The federal government had held down inflation and financed part of the war by selling victory bonds to a patriotic public, so billions of dollars were sitting in the banks just waiting to be redeemed and spent. Factories quickly switched from wartime to peacetime production, employment levels remained high, and a boom began in constructing new houses and filling both them and old ones with new appliances like fridges. New suburbs spread around the cities creating another boom as the entire infrastructure of roads, sewers, hydro and telephones, schools, parks, stores and shopping centres had to be built.

The war ended on August 6, 1945, just as another federal-provincial conference was failing to reach agreement on how to restructure the country's post war economy. Peacetime brought no peace to federal-provincial relations. Ottawa was determined to keep the temporary taxation powers that the provinces had willingly transferred for the prosecution of the war. And it was determined to use that additional revenue to develop comprehensive programs for pensions and welfare.

This was coupled with the idea that the federal government would use its fiscal and monetary power to balance out booms and depression. That was similar to what

Hepburn had so strongly advocated throughout the Depression. But Drew had his own program, the Twenty Two Points, and he had no intention of allowing federal programs to overshadow his own, not in areas of jurisdiction that were clearly provincial. The net effect was that when the Wartime Tax Agreement expired in 1947, Ontario revived most of its pre-war taxes, and refused to participate in Ottawa's new welfare state.

The post-war boom brought another old political-economic problem to the fore – the potential shortage of electric power. Wartime demand had been met by a combination of rationing, building coal-fired plants, and diverting water from rivers that flowed north to James Bay into the Great Lakes to augment Niagara power. Drew decided to tackle two major issues, the development of more power on three rivers, which would cost $400 million, and the old problem of converting Ontario's 25 cycle electricity system to the North American standard of 60 cycles. That would cost $100 million because industry and some seven million appliances had to be converted. With the post-war boom in full swing, the change could no longer be postponed.

It was a well-established practice to call elections every three years, so Drew decided to ask for a mandate for his new energy strategy. Once more, however, liquor control became a major issue. The laws were again far out of date, but a shrinking minority of prohibitionists still regarded the liquor control regime as the most important issue in the province. Drew passed a law that allowed the five largest cities to have liquor, wine and beer sold and consumed in hotels, restaurants, lounges, pubs, and taverns. Other municipalities could introduce the same relaxation if 60% of the voters approved of it by referendum.

This measure along with three years of good government, hydro development, and increased spending on schools put the Conservatives in a good position. The adjustment to peace had gone smoothly, and the province was booming Drew had provided good government. He had stood up to Ottawa even if he had not won many victories. The Liberals were still in disarray, and the CCF lacked leadership. Drew easily swept to victory on June 7, 1948, with 53 seats. The CCF regained their position as Opposition with 21 seats while the liberals fell to 13.

Although the Conservatives swept back to power, Drew was not amongst them. In a show of arrogant bravado, he had decided to run in one of the driest of all constituencies, and he was personally defeated. He had tired of provincial politics anyway, and saw a bright future leading the federal Conservatives. He was perhaps the sixth Ontario premier to be tempted by the lure of the federal Prime Minister's office, but he was the first to actually try to make the transition. His five predecessors had read it correctly. Defending Ontario's interests had meant opposing the interests of other provinces, a legacy Drew could not escape as a national political leader.

Drew had dominated his cabinet, but there was one clearly outstanding minister, his quiet, unassuming, un-ambitious, and superb Treasurer, Leslie Frost. Frost was an affable small-town lawyer from Lindsay, who made a point of emphasizing his unpretentious rural roots and folksy ways. It was good politics because most Ontarians did not care much for arrogant city slickers like Drew. But behind that smile lurked a tough, honest, highly-intelligent, authoritarian, no nonsense leader with extremely good political instincts, combined with a talent for administration and building good relationships. Frost liked to be called "Old Man Ontario"; others called him the "Silver Fox". He had no enemies in cabinet or in the party, and after enough people had urged him to run, he agreed. He won on the first ballet, became the province's 16th premier in 1949, and easily won the elections of 1951, 1955 and 59.

Frost saw politics as the art of the possible, not as a political battle with a "winner-take-all" outcome. He saw the opposition, including the Communists, as politically responsible though somewhat misguided citizens who might on occasion develop a good policy worth stealing and implementing. He saw the political-economic situation as a sort of wheel – more government programs created more jobs which led to more production and spending, which led to higher wages and more taxes, which permitted his government to do more spending to produce more infrastructure. His job was to keep the wheel spinning smoothly, and make the economy bigger and better.

After administering the province for two years, Frost called an election for November 22, 1951 to get his own mandate as premier. The province was booming and experiencing harmonious relations between the political parties and with Ottawa, and there were no scandals to arouse opposition and media attention. Many of the programs outlined in the famous Twenty Two Points had been implemented or were underway, and taxes were low. The opposition parties were still in search of leaders, popular policies, and weaknesses in the government's armour. Frost swept to his first mandate, with 79 seats on 48% of the vote. The Liberal vote increased from 29 to 31%, but they lost six seats for a total of seven. The CCF vote fell from 27% to 19%, leaving them with two seats instead of 13. It was one of the most decisive victories in Ontario's history.

Frost viewed the federal government as a fact of life that Ontario had to deal with, it had imperatives and policies, and he had to work with it to minimize the damage it could do to Ontario and to maximize the good. Luck was on his side, for at about the same time, Mackenzie King was replaced by the more pragmatic Louis St. Laurent. Frost immediately wrote St. Laurent to congratulate him, and offered to meet so that the two new heads of government could discuss areas for cooperation. After the stormy years of Mackenzie King's endless fights with premiers from coast to coast, the letter must have come as a great relief. St. Laurent immediately agreed, and the two leaders changed the relationship from confrontation to cooperation. One of the first examples was the 1952 agreement on tax sharing by which Ontario allowed Ottawa to collect income and other taxes and turn over a fixed amount to Queen's Park for five years. In 1957, the agreement was amended in Ontario's favour and extended.

For Ontario, the importance of this relationship was enormous. Frost and St. Laurent built the two foundations for the province's continued prosperity in the second half of the twentieth century. Those foundations were the St.. Lawrence Seaway and the Trans-Canada Pipeline. For decades there had been discussions about building a seaway to carry ocean-going ships past the St. Lawrence rapids and on to Toronto, Thunder Bay and Chicago. At the same time as those canals were built, a dam could harness the water power not needed for navigation. The plan had been postponed repeatedly because of the conflicting interests of the four governments which would have to be involved.

Now Ontario had run out of alternative sources of energy and was finally ready to make the investment in the St. Lawrence. Ottawa had finally abandoned the attempt to use its responsibility for navigation to gain control of power production. The arrangement called for Ottawa to build the canals and Ontario to build the dam and the power plants. New York State needed power, so it was amenable to sharing the costs. The seaway would provide stiff competition for railways, and railway interests had convinced the American government to oppose it. Frost and St. Laurent were in no mood for further delay, and said they would unilaterally build the seaway and dam on the Canadian side if the Americans chose to stay out. Faced with a fait accompli, and with Canada getting all the power plus control of the seaway, Washington decided to join the project.

Construction began in 1954 and the seaway opened in 1959. It involved the construction of the massive dam at Iroquois, plus the canals and power house. It required the flooding of 100 square miles of land and 200 farms, the relocation of 6,000 people, and the moving of dozens of historic buildings to the permanent outdoor museum of Upper Canada Village. Ontario gained adequate hydro power for two more decades of growth. Ocean-going ships could sail to Toronto and other lake ports, cutting the cost of imports, and making Ontario's exports more competitive internationally. It opened about the same time as the four-lane Highway 401 from Windsor to Montreal. That was part of a system of super-highways including the 400 running north from Toronto, the Queen Elizabeth Way (QEW) around the western end of Lake Ontario, and the Queensway through Ottawa, plus massive bridges over Hamilton Harbour, over the St. Lawrence, between Windsor and Detroit, and between the Canadian and American cities of Sault Ste Marie.

The second pillar of Ontario's new energy policy, and of federal-provincial co-operation, was a trans-Canada natural gas pipeline. It was a new concept, with equally difficult problems to overcome. Ontario needed a secure and adequate supply of natural gas to heat homes and factories. Alberta had a surplus, and was willing to sell it. Canadian companies wanted to export Alberta gas to the northwest United States, and import American gas into central Canada from Texas. C.D. Howe, the powerful federal minister of Trade and Commerce, agreed. Economically this made sense, but Ontario had major concerns – the Texas gas might not be reliable, and it would only be available in the southwest part of the province which might be too small a market. On the other hand, supplying Ontario with Alberta gas meant building the pipeline across the Precambrian Shield where, like the railways before, the costs of construction would be high and the local markets small.

Fortunately again Frost and St. Laurent worked well together, and the decision was made to build an all-Canadian pipeline. The Ontario and federal governments would pay the cost of the line through northern Ontario. The two governments forced the private companies to form a single company – Trans-Canada Pipelines

– to build and operate it, including the distribution network in Ontario and on to Montreal. It was a massive engineering and financial effort, and it touched off mini-economic booms as it snaked across the north, just like railways had done in an earlier age. By 1959 Ontario homes and factories had the energy security they needed – heating and electricity were guaranteed.

The two governments co-operated on another energy front. In World War II Canada had made a major contribution to the development of the atomic bomb, supplying uranium, science and engineering. That work had been done in Ontario. Uranium could also be used to produce electricity. That was a provincial responsibility, and the two levels of government could have fought over it as previous ones had fought over hydroelectricity. But Ottawa did not insist on a role in Ontario's control of nuclear-produced electricity, and the two governments co-operated with the development of uranium mines, technology and nuclear power plants. The St. Lawrence Seaway had harnessed the last great hydro potential in the province, and nuclear energy increasingly filled the growing demand of the 1980s and 1990s.

While these giant projects dominated the politics and economics of the period, and were of major importance to people throughout the province, Frost found time to deal with other issues. One was the fact that urban sprawl around Toronto had completely overgrown the nineteenth-century municipal borders, creating a single metropolitan area with a dozen, small, fragmented competing municipalities with varying tax rates, each one incapable of providing coordinated and comprehensive government. The provincial government created the Municipality of Metropolitan Toronto with a single regional council having responsibility for police, fire, transportation, water, sewage and parks.

Frost also addressed the difficult issue of hospital insurance. His own view was that private enterprise should look after the majority of people, and government should only intervene to help those who were in need. But for years pressure had been building for government to provide a comprehensive program, which the federal government was eager to do. Ontario resisted the trend for over a decade, but finally agreed in 1959 to a 50-50 federal provincial program entitled the Ontario Health Care Insurance Plan. Ontario also agreed to the federal government's establishing old age pensions for anyone over 70, while it instituted pensions for poorer Ontarians over 65.

Like every premier before him, Frost faced pressure from the Protestant churches to use the power of government to enforce religious morality. In particular they wanted a crack down on bars frequented by prostitutes, which the government did. There was pressure from the public to ease liquor regulations, but the government resisted it. It was illegal to advertise alcohol on radio or TV, but the government failed in its attempts to protect its morally-weak citizens from the influences of such advertising on American media. The churches pressured the government to ban gambling at horse races. Gambling was a federal responsibility, so Frost simply banned horse racing after 7pm.

During this period the population mix of Ontario changed quite significantly. After World War II, British immigrants continued to arrive, along with a new wave of migration from Germany, and a steady trickle from the Netherlands. They were outnumbered by a huge wave of migration from southern Europe, mainly Italian, but also including Greek and Portuguese migrants. They changed forever the character of Ontario's cities, the architecture, ways of entertainment, and especially the restaurants. Political upheaval in Eastern Europe produced an influx of Hungarians, Yugoslavs and Czechs. In the 1960s Canada relaxed restrictions that had favoured white immigrants, and Ontario benefited from the arrival of Asians, especially Chinese, South Asian and Philippino, and of Caribbean blacks. Across the province the proportion with British or French backgrounds declined, and Toronto in particular evolved from being a bastion of White Anglo-Saxon Protestant values in the 1940s to becoming one of the most racially and religiously "multicultural" cities in the world.

In the Frost years Ontario experienced the greatest boom in its history, recording real economic growth above inflation of over 4% per annum. It can be argued that the 1950s was a major watershed in Ontario's history. In that decade the average Ontarian became rich, certainly far richer that his parents. Salaries and wages rose quickly, and working women added a second income to households. Most families had cars which greatly reduced the time it took to get around. Households acquired labour-saving devices from fridges to dish washers to power lawn mowers. People had more money and more leisure time to watch their new TV or to travel, and travel by air became common. It was a period of unprecedented prosperity, security and optimism.

Frost's philosophy was that the government's job was to keep the wheel of economic growth turning, to solve problems, to ensure energy security, to modernize education and every other branch of government, to build the super highways and provincial arteries, and to work with whomever he had to in order to achieve those goals, including the federal government. He was exceptional in his ability to achieve his goals. He won the dull 1955 election with 84 out of 98 seats, to the Liberals 11 and the CCF's three. In June 1959 another dull election campaign produced the sixth straight victory for the Conservatives, with 71 out of 98 seats. Later, with the party and the province is superb shape, he announced his retirement so the party could renew itself. And he retired to Lindsay where, as he never tired of saying, his heart had always been.

Chapter Nine
John Robarts and the Welfare State, 1961 – 1971

Premier Frost left both province and party in superb shape, and seven candidates entered the campaign to replace him. John Robarts won the prize, somewhat of a surprise given that he had only been promoted to cabinet two years earlier. He was well qualified and liked, and while the other six candidates had more experience, they had also made more enemies. Powerful members of the party were determined to stop two of them, while Robarts was the second choice of many delegates. Robarts ran a good campaign, avoided personal attacks, and cultivated delegates and the media.

Luck was also a factor. He was minister of education at a time when the baby boom had reached the high schools, and he had travelled all over the province opening new schools. Naturally, when there is a cabinet minister in town, the local party brass and media come out to meet him. He was also a good minister, promoting many changes, pushing for the development of more technical and vocational schools to produce the skilled workers the province needed. He was innovative, forceful, imaginative, and successful, and he had negotiated an agreement whereby the federal government would be paying 75% of the costs of the technical courses. He won on the sixth ballot, to become the province's 16th premier, a job he would hold for a decade.

John Parmenter Robarts was a lawyer from London, a Second World War II vet, and an experienced local politician before being elected to Queen's Park in 1951. Though not as handsome as Drew, he cut a good figure – tall, smiling, affable, and confident, with a wide circle of friends from different vocations. He was a heavy drinker, loved parties and enjoying good music in Toronto's night clubs. Robarts immediately assembled an excellent cabinet, giving his defeated rivals the portfolios they asked for. Ideologically he was a "progressive conservative" who believed that nothing should be changed unless it had to be, and then only slowly and carefully.

While Robarts had great respect for Frost the politician, he had serious reservations about Frost the administrator. Basically, Frost ran the government the way it had been managed since Confederation, with himself ultimately in charge of everything, intervening in ministries, even interrupting ministers when they were answering questions in the Assembly. But he had no bureaucratic system, and government had grown infinitely more complex since the war. Robarts prided himself on being a "management man", the chairman of the board. He provided general direction and coordination to his ministers, and let them get on with their responsibilities. Then he created a system of committees to provide the bureaucratic support and specific coordination for his rapidly-growing government. He immediately re-organized the premier's office, including the public relations section.

While Frost was overly dominant, Robarts at first was too trusting of his ministers. This became apparent when Attorney General Fred Cass introduced some amendments to the Police Act. One of them allowed the police to force witnesses to give testimony during private interrogation. Officials assured the Attorney General that there was no problem with this additional power, and Cass did not raise it when the bill was discussed in cabinet. But the bill provided the type of power that police wield in dictatorships, and Cass told the press he thought the power was drastic. There was a media frenzy over the issue and over a minister seeming to doubt his own legislation. Cabinet was divided, backbenchers threatened to quit the party, and the opposition forced an embarrassed Robarts to delete the clause. Cass resigned and a chastened Robarts began to exercise stricter control over his government.

In 1962 the four-year old recession came to an end, and Ontario entered another period of rapid economic growth, maintaining its position as the richest Canadian province. Robarts set out to complete Drew's famous Twenty Two Point agenda, the virtual creation of a twentieth-century welfare state. Unfortunately for Robarts, the newly-elected federal Liberal government of Lester Pearson decided to do the same for the whole country, and it did not care if the issues were in provincial jurisdiction. Robarts tenure as premier, and Ontario politics throughout the 1960s, would be dominated by the battle for control of the welfare state.

This time Ontario would lose all the big battles, and it is important to understand why. First, in World War II, Ontario and the other provinces had transferred much of their taxing power to Ottawa as a temporary measure. After the war, Ottawa had violated the understanding, and kept those powers and revenue. In the post-war period, Ontario had not fought hard enough to get them back, and was not therefore as powerful financially in 1962 as it had been before World War II. Second, Premier Frost had entered a tax-sharing deal with Louis St Laurent whereby Ottawa collected provincial taxes and gave back a per capita grant. Frost had been warned that the government that collects taxes controls them, but he ignored that advice.

Third, while the federal government believed that it was completely unacceptable for a province to interfere in federal jurisdiction as Hepburn had done in 1940, it saw nothing wrong with interfering in any provincial responsibilities. As Canadian nationalism grew, Canadians outside Quebec tended to accept that interpretation of the Constitution. By the 1960s, the federal government had also discovered the winning strategy for invading provincial jurisdiction. It was to design a program for the provinces, allocate part of its financial surplus to it, and offer the program on a 50-50 shared-cost basis. The provincial governments then had the choice of joining that program or seeing the portion of federal taxes collected in their province spent elsewhere. Politically, they could not resist. Then once the public had grown used to the new service or program, Ottawa would abandon it, leaving the provinces to pay the costs while Ottawa launched another shared-cost program.

This was the background to Robarts' battle with Ottawa over hospital insurance. Private companies in Ontario had long offered hospital insurance to those who could pay the premiums. To Robarts, all that government should do was develop a program to cover those too poor to participate in the private plans. Ottawa, however, wanted a public plan with national-standards that would cover everyone. Poorer provinces were supportive because national standards would be better than what they could afford, and richer provinces like Ontario would pay for the difference.

Robarts had two other problems with federal hospital insurance. In Ontario the insurance companies used the premiums to invest in the provincial economy. If a federal scheme replaced the private ones, the federal government could and likely would use the money for national programs, such as addressing regional disparities in other parts of Canada. Robarts' other problem was that the federal proposals were not detailed, the studies behind them had not been made public, and there had been no thorough study or debate on the issues. For years, Robarts fought the federal program, but eventually he had to accept it.

Another battle developed over pensions. In July, 1963, Ottawa announced the Canada Pension Plan, a single system into which every employed Canadian and his or her employer would contribute, a program to be transferable between companies and between provinces. Ontario had been working on a plan for three years; Ottawa for only three months, and the implications of Ottawa's plan were far from clear. Robarts was not opposed to a federal plan providing it was sufficiently flexible to accommodate Ontario's. He told Pearson that the federal government could not pass legislation on a matter of provincial jurisdiction. Pearson ignored him.

A federal-provincial conference was scheduled for November, 1963, to discuss the issue. Ottawa produced a poorly-drafted proposal. Quebec made clear that it was going to have its own pension program, and shared the details of that program with the others. It was immediately clear that the Quebec Plan was far superior to the federal one. In addition to providing secure pensions, the Quebec plan called for collecting funds immediately for pensions that would be paid decades later. In the interval, the Quebec government would invest that money in the Quebec economy. The federal government recognized the superiority of the Quebec plan, and basically substituted it for its own. Robarts fought against the plan for years, but eventually felt compelled to accept it. One unforeseen result of the debate was that Robarts realized how superior the Quebec civil service was to Ontario's, and he launched an overhaul, expansion and modernization of his bureaucracy.

The next major battle was over medicare. Saskatchewan had introduced public medicare, and had made it work. Other provinces were moving towards similar programs, and in 1962 Robarts said Ontario would create its own program. The federal government decided that Canada should have a single system, standardized from coast-to-coast. It could be administered by the provinces, and Ottawa would pay a major share, but only if the plan was portable, comprehensive, universal and government-run. Ontario had private plans which did not meet these criteria, and by 1965 had a government plan to cover those too poor to participate in the private ones. Ontario did not believe that a national plan was needed since everyone was covered by existing private or government plans. It vehemently objected to the federal government's attempt to impose such a massive plan in an area of provincial jurisdiction.

On July 27, 1965, Robarts strongly condemned Ottawa for failure to consult the provinces and for using its financial strength to force provinces to accept its dictates. Ontario's doctors supported Robarts, but the opposition parties did not. Robarts argued that the discussion of medicare should be postponed until the completion of several major studies that were underway. He asked Ottawa to share the studies it had done, but Ottawa refused. He did not believe Ontario could afford the plan, and was upset that it would lead to the cancellation of private plans that had worked well for decades. Robarts was also furious that Ottawa was proposing programs for technical and vocational education without consultation, as it had previously done for a program to help municipalities, another area of clear provincial jurisdiction.

Ottawa was also trying to abandon other shared-cost programs that imposed federal standards, which would add to the province's costs. Ottawa was, in effect, jumping in and out of provincial responsibilities without any overall plan, imposing conditions, and cherry-picking where and when it would get involved or withdraw, to the consternation of provinces which were trying to plan coherently for all of their responsibilities. And when Ontario asked the federal government to yield tax points so that provinces could raise funds for the new federally-imposed programs, Ottawa's response was that Ontario could raise its level of taxation, which Robarts was forced to do in his 1965 budget.

By 1966 seven of 10 provinces opposed the federal medicare plan. Public opinion outside Quebec was in favour of the single plan for the rest-of-Canada, including the Ontario Liberals and especially the NDP. Robarts decided not to join the federal plan, but the poorer provinces joined it, and Ottawa announced its implementation on July 1, 1968. It then cancelled its other shared-cost medical programs including cancer care and medical research, putting more pressure on Ontario to join. It also imposed a 2% surtax on income tax to pay for the plan, confirming Robart's analysis of its costs..

Again Robarts was furious because Ontario had been planning such a tax increase, had informed Ottawa, and now could not implement it because of taxpayer resistance. Ontarians realized that they were losing health programs and paying for the national plan. Given public opinion and the state of the province's finances, Robarts was forced to sign on, and the Ontario Health Insurance Plan, OHIP, came into effect on October 1, 1969.

While these battles were dominating the headlines and leading Ontarians into the current systems that characterize their pensions and health service, the province was experiencing one of the greatest economic booms in its history. It was driven especially by the automobile industry. A free trade deal with the United States, called Autopact, helped make Ontario a centre of the booming North America automobile industry. The 1960s was the first decade when most adults owned cars. As cities expanded into the countryside, the automobile became the essential means of transportation, and the suburbs were designed for them - sprawling clusters of curved, treeless streets, thousands of houses whose architecture reflected only a dozen different designs, with huge indoor shopping centres protected from the Canadian weather, supplemented by unattractive strip malls, and the usual collection of schools, churches, parks, arenas and sports facilities. Linking the cities were the super highways, always expanding in distance and width, with giant expressways connecting the various parts of Toronto to the city centre which was increasingly seen by its denizens as the centre of Canada.

The population mushroomed from 6.2 million to 7.7 million. It continued to evolve – more people in larger cities, a declining proportion of the population from either British or French stock, more immigrants especially from East Asia, South

Asia, the Caribbean, the Middle East, and Africa. The religious make-up was changing rapidly, with Protestants a declining majority, Catholics growing to 35%, and
sizeable minorities of Sikhs, Hindus and Muslims beginning to make a mark. Old
organizations like the Orange Lodge had almost disappeared, and with them the old-
world quarrels their ancestors had brought from Europe.

The new society was more tolerant, more open, more progressive and more complex. Some old questions took on new dimensions – if Catholics could have government-supported separate schools, why not Muslims, Jews and others? Other attitudes
were changing, particularly that of youth, who revolted against their parents' values,
both good and bad. That wave of protest also led to more relaxed liquor laws, more
concern for the environment and a very different kind of popular music and dance.
The birth rate continued to fall rapidly, the population aged, and schools became
underutilized while the demand for senior's homes could not be met.

In this society, Robarts and the Conservative government ruled seemingly ef-
fortlessly. In spite of his complaints about inadequate tax-sharing by the federal government, the economic boom produced enormous revenues for the provincial government. The civil service doubled in size, and government spending quadrupled
in the decade, much of it going into the new infrastructure around and between the
exploding cities. That infrastructure included twenty community colleges to fill the
gap between high school and the universities, and four new universities, Laurentian
in Sudbury, Brock in St. Catharine's, Trent in Peterborough and York in Downsview,
plus the upgrading of Windsor, Lakehead and Waterloo to university status.

Robarts was extremely concerned with the challenges posed to Canada's unity
in the 1960s, and believed that the government of the largest province had a particularly important role in promoting unity and solving national problems. He developed excellent relations with the new Liberal premier of Quebec, Jean Lesage, and
made strenuous efforts to let Quebecers know that Ontario respected their views.
One of the reasons he opposed federal intrusion into provincial jurisdiction was that
it created disunity between levels of government and between provinces and regions.
Limitations on the "rights" of Franco-Ontarians were still a sore point in Quebec,
and Robarts extended support to Catholic schools for Grades 9 and 10 and increased
French language instruction.

Robarts called an election for September 25, 1963. The Conservatives hadn't
been able to think of a theme or even an excuse, but Robarts had been working on a
speech to end the current Assembly session. After drinking into the wee hours with
his cronies, he went back to his office and re-read the Speech from the Throne that
had introduced the session three years earlier. As he read it, he realized his government had honoured every promise. The next day he re-read that speech in the Assembly, only at the end of every promise he said slowly and loudly "Done". Conservative
MLAs took up the theme, shouting "Done" along with him.

The Conservatives had their campaign theme – a government that fulfilled all its
promises. The opposition Liberals supported the federal pension plan proposal and
tried unsuccessfully to make crime an issue. The CCF, now under the name of New

Democratic Party or NDP, was still struggling to build an effective party. Excellent organization and good candidates helped produce another Conservative landslide, with an increase in the Conservatives popular vote to 48% and an increase of six seats to 77. Both Liberals and NDP gained two seats in the larger Assembly of 108 seats, with 23 and seven respectively.

In 1967, the centennial of Confederation, Robarts decided to host a meeting of premiers to celebrate the work their predecessors had done a century before and to discuss the current state of the nation. It was called the Confederation of Tomorrow. The conference show-cased Toronto's growth and importance as it was held in the 54th floor of the tallest building in Canada. The conference was the first to be televised. It was not designed to address any problems, just to exchange views and get better acquainted without the presence of a federal agenda or politicians. Robarts saw it as a success, and continued for the rest of his premiership to try to bridge differences and promote unity as he did with a major contribution to Expo in Montreal.

With the country basking in the glory of the centennial celebrations, Robarts decided to ask for a new mandate on October 17. The province was prosperous, the government had done a reasonable job in handling issues and responding to new problems and challenges like the environment. The government's policy was more of the same. The Liberals were starting to re-build but were still weak. This time, however, the NDP was well organized, with better leadership, and a good platform. The Conservative popular vote declined from 49% to 42%, costing them eight seats but maintaining a majority of 69 out of the enlarged Assembly of 117. The Liberals lost four percentage points but managed to remain the official opposition with 27 seats. The NDP picked up votes from both Conservatives and Liberals to increase their vote total from five to 25 and their number of seats from seven to 20. Robarts was safe for another four years.

The near-continuous economic and demographic boom since World War II and the enormous growth of cities was making local government obsolete, especially in the eyes of the bureaucracy in Toronto. There were, they thought, too many little school boards and municipal jurisdictions. In December 1968 the government announced the amalgamation of a number of municipalities into 10 major regional governments, uniting the cities of Fort William and Port Arthur into Thunder Bay, creating Ottawa-Carleton, and Sudbury and seven other amalgamated cities in southern Ontario, each to have a population of over 150,000. These new boards would have responsibility for regional issues like transportation, police and fire service.

However desirable in theory, the issue was very badly managed in practice. Thousands of citizens were proud of the contribution they made to society by serving in local government, and they believed such government was highly democratic and re-sponsible to local ratepayers and parents. They distrusted, perhaps with cause, well-paid civil servants in distant Toronto, with their incomprehensible talk about modern administration. The party did not seem to have done its home-work either, because local government was the bedrock of the Conservative party. The government bungled the timing, introducing regional government on the argument that it was more efficient at the same time as property taxes were being increased because of rising costs. The angry outgoing boards decided to blow their budgets, so the incoming ones inherited bare cupboards and had to raise taxes. A full-blown tax revolt began to develop.

The government was forced to slow the process and spend some effort explaining it. The fact that this had been done at the beginning suggested that the Conservative dynasty might be dying of old age. That was confirmed when it lost a by-election in a very traditional Tory seat. Robarts, however, knew how to respond. The government had blundered in introducing sweeping reform, so it switched to micro-reforms targeted at specific groups, like renewal of the harbour front in Toronto, lowering the drinking age, and building the Ontario Science Centre. Robarts went on a diet and cut back on his drinking. He re-organized the Cabinet, promoting young and energetic ministers. Tax refunds and grants to municipalities bought off much of the discontent. But other issues were festering, like anti-Americanism and the environment, and other parties were making a generational change in their leadership. On December, 1971, at the age of 64, John Robarts decided it was time for the Conservative Party to renew itself as it had repeatedly done since 1939, and he headed into retirement at his family home in London.

Chapter Ten
Bill Davis and the Big Blue Machine, 1971 – 1985

Bill Davis was the next of the Tory premiers who dominated Ontario from 1942 to 1985. After Oliver Mowat, Davis was the longest serving premier in Ontario's history. The convention that elected Davis was, however, a cliff-hanger. Davis was the favourite of the Troy establishment, popular with everyone, and an experienced minister. But he seemed to take his election for granted, and ran a dull, uninspired campaign. He was overweight, and delivered a series of dull speeches, both in content and in emotion. He smoked cigars, which was not exactly the image the party wanted. He came first on the first ballot, first on the second, first on the third, and won the fourth by just 44 votes. In short, Davis almost lost it, and he learned an important lesson about complacency.

Davis was raised in Brampton, the son of a wealthy lawyer who married the daughter of a wealthy shoe manufacturer. He went to the best schools, and enjoyed sports and music. The family was strict Presbyterian and Methodist, and frowned on drinking and parties. Davis found it difficult to relax with people, or indeed to relax anywhere except at his family cottage. He was quiet, courteous and pleasant, set up a successful law practice in Brampton, and ran for local government. He was the youngest candidate ever sent to a national Progressive Conservative convention, and was elected to the Assembly in 1959.

He was the youngest person ever appointed to an Ontario Cabinet, becoming minister of education in the Robarts government. That was the base Robarts himself had used to seize the premiership, and Davis followed his mentor. Education was high profile, growing dramatically, full of challenges and new schools to open. In the eyes of the Conservative party, Davis made an excellent job of the ministry because he was shrewd, smart, energetic, ambitious and open. He was definitely not a fiscal conservative – spending on education rose 450% during his decade as minister. The fact that he was dull may help explain why he almost lost the leadership, and it became somewhat of a public joke. Asked about it once he is reported to have said that in politics "bland works".

"Brampton Bill" moved rapidly to put his imprint on government. Like Robarts before him, Davis assigned all of the defeated leadership candidates to the most important portfolios. The Conservative Party was, after all, a family. It was the right thing to do in terms of the quality of the candidates, their egos, and team-building. Perhaps more importantly, he hired a number of professionals in advertising and polling to remake party organization, image and public relations. In an age of television and instant gratification, of short messages to the media and of short attention-spans by the public, managing the media had become enormously important. Davis was in tune with these developments. These media and organizational whiz-kids kids would become the basis of the legend of the unbeatable "Big Blue Machine", blue being the political colour of the Conservative party. One of the first things they did was re-create Davis, without the cigars and excess weight. Eliminating "bland" was a more difficult challenge.

The new premier faced the same problem as all his predecessors, namely how to escape from the shadow of a predecessor who had dominated the province for a decade. Fortunately, an opportunity presented itself. Toronto had been building expressways to move the ever increasing number of cars in and out of the increasingly congested city centre. Each expressway required the destruction of houses, apartments, businesses, neighbourhoods, or parks, and each one contributed to growing pollution and traffic jams at the entrances and exits. Resistance had been growing, and the new expressway on Spadina mobilized even more opposition. Suddenly, Davis made a speech in the Assembly saying cities were for people, not cars, and shut down the proposed expressway. It was a brilliant tactical move, identifying the new premier as a man of decision, a man who listens to the people, a man who does things differently, and a friend of the environment. It was also mainly hype – his government continued with massive spending on highways with the odd sop to public transit.

In his first administration Davis introduced over 130 bills to modernize Ontario. He established a ministry of environment, created a new airline, Nordair, to service the north, established preferences for Canadian companies in response to growing nationalism, showed he was "hip" by lowering the voting and drinking age to 18, and showed he was responsible by making it more difficult for teenagers to go on welfare. He then called an election for October 21, 1971, to see if the people of Ontario approved the Progressive Conservative Party's selection of Davis as their premier.

The outcome was never in doubt, and the Conservatives had proven once more that they grasped the secret of passing power from one generation to the next. Robarts was a memory, Frost a shadow from the past, and Drew had faded into history. Davis was the new incarnation of Progressive Conservative Ontario, with an overwhelming majority of 78, up nine from the last election. The Liberals had sacrificed seven of those new Tory seats, leaving them with 20, and the NDP had lost two leaving them still in third place with 19.

Davis' second term began, however, with scandals rather than achievement. Some of them reflected the type of decisions that politicians make when they have grown too used to power and start to cross the line into the abuse of position, like using government airplanes to take their families on holidays. One minister had to resign when it was discovered that he was involved in a company that did business with the government. Several MPPs were accused of real estate speculation using privileged information.

As a result, Davis brought in the toughest legislation in Canada on the separation of minister's public and business affairs. However, the scandals and hints of scandal continued. There was an accusation that a friend of the premier had received a contract from Ontario Hydro without competition. The investigation validated those facts, but found no evidence that the contract was awarded because of the personal relationship. Attorney General George Kerr was accused of taking campaign funds from a company that was involved in construction in Hamilton. Kerr had to resign for the duration of the investigation, but was reinstated when the accusations proved groundless. Another minister who made money off a questionable real estate transaction was not so lucky.

Davis' first administration also faced a major strike by the province's teachers. This was a period of very high inflation, and many employees were growing poorer as costs rose faster than wages. It was also a period when groups such as teachers and civil servants were starting to act like factory unions, backing their demands with real or threatened strikes. In December, 1973, almost 8,000 teachers backed up their wage demands with the threat of resigning. The province's 100,000 teachers threatened a one-day walk out. Twenty thousand of them demonstrated at Queen's Park. The government had introduced legislation to make it illegal for teachers to resign, but had to back down. Davis said he would ban strikes by teachers, but had to back down again. By the spring the government had given teachers the right to strike, and both teachers and school boards had the right to take their disputes to either voluntary or binding arbitration.

During this period the government lost a number of by-elections in for m e r l y safe seats. Davis responded with legislation to raise the standards of politics in general. The financial affairs of parties had to be audited and made public annually. Donations were limited to $4,000, and the names of anyone donating over $100 had to be made public. Advertising during campaigns was limited. Ontario caught up to some other provinces by appointing its first ombudsman. The 1975 budget suggested that an election was coming – the sales tax was reduced from 7% to 5%, the province would pay for drugs for senior citizens, and assistance was given to help people buy their first house. Energy prices were frozen for 90 days, forcing companies to absorb rapidly rising costs. Davis and his ministers took to the highways to announce funding for hundreds of local projects.

An important element in the Big Blue Machine, as the Conservative organization came to be known, was public opinion polling. It revealed that the public was responding positively to the government's activities, with the Conservatives gaining at the expense of the Liberals. The NDP was making major gains on the strength of its demand for rent control, an issue of serious concern during a period of rapid inflation. Davis called the election for September 18, 1975. The NDP succeeded in making rent control one of the main issues, and that put the Conservatives on the defensive. Every day NDP leader Stephen Lewis gave the media examples of people who were reduced to poverty as mean and insensitive landlords jacked up their rent.

It did not matter that these might be isolated cases in a population of 8,000,000, all of whom were facing rising costs. It did not matter that many tenants could afford increased rent and many homeowners were hard pressed to pay their increased costs, including renewing mortgages at far higher interest rates. Conservative polling showed that rising rents was hurting their chances of re-election, and Davis announced rent control just days before the election. The Housing Minister did not know the announcement was coming, and ministers issued contradictory statements on how it would be implemented. Rent control violated the party's free enterprise ideology, and its adoption violated the normal process of developing policy by consensus.

The polls still showed a very tight race, but in the televised leaders' debate, Davis did well and Liberal leader Robert Nixon did not. The electorate decided that the Conservatives should be reduced to minority status and that the NDP should be the opposition. The Conservative popular vote fell from 44% to 35%, its seat total falling from 78 to 51 in an enlarged Assembly of 125 seats. The NDP's percentage of popular vote increased less than 2%, but the concentration on rent control paid off in urban constituencies giving them 19 more seats for a total of 38. The Liberals increased their share of the popular vote by 5% and their number of seats by 15, to 35. The NDP's success indicated that Davis' death-bed conversion to rent control had failed, but the province was now saddled with a policy that discouraged investment in rental housing which further pushed up prices. One result of that was that government had to subsidize the building of new rental accommodation.

A number of Conservatives felt they had lost votes because the party had moved too far to the left, unsuccessfully chasing the voters who normally supported the opposition with policies like rent control. So Davis moved to the right, appointing several conservative ministers and clamping down on the massive increases in social spending that had gone on for a decade. Being in a minority position the party also kept its political machine and organization in top condition. They also decided to make the maximum increase in rents 8% rather than the 6% they had previously announced, another clear move to the political right. The NDP and Liberals demanded that it be 6%. The government made it an issue of confidence and was defeated. In the election of June 9, 1977, the Conservatives took votes and seats from both opposition parties, rising from 51 to 58 seats, slightly short of a majority. The Liberals lost one seat for a total of 34 but the NDP lost five for a total of 33. Once more the Liberals were the official Opposition, with dreams of forming the government in the not too distant future.

One of the biggest challenges for Davis was his attempt to protect the province from rising international oil prices. Due to a combination of circumstances, the price of oil shot up in the early 1970s, carrying with it the price of gasoline and natural gas, essential expenditures for every family and factory in the world. Canada produced much of the oil and gas it needed, and Davis believed that Ontario should not have to pay international prices. That meant that the provinces in western Canada that produced oil and gas should sell it to Central Canada for much less than they could sell it in the United States, basically, that Alberta should subsidize Ontario.

Albertans saw the issue quite differently. They had always sold all of their exports at world prices, and when those prices fell, Alberta suffered. Ontario had always sold its minerals, like nickel, to the rest of Canada at world prices, never subsidized ones. Indeed, Ontario's industry had been built in part by the National Policy, whereby Albertans paid up to 30% more than American prices for manufactured goods from Central Canada. Davis' demand that Alberta subsidize Ontario consumers and industry thus provoked a negative and bitter response from western Canada.

Davis, however, had an important ally in this dispute, namely the federal Liberal government of Pierre Trudeau. Its power base was in central and eastern Canada, and it had few seats to win or lose in the west. Forcing the west to subsidize Ontario was questionable economics and terrible politics in terms of national unity, but it was good politics in terms of re-electing the federal Liberal government. For one of the few times ever, Ontario and Ottawa found themselves on the same side of a federal-provincial dispute, and Davis became Trudeau's greatest supporter, and sometimes the only supporter, amongst the provincial premiers.

In the battles over energy pricing, taxation and control of resources Davis and Trudeau were in almost complete agreement, and they made a bitter political enemy of Alberta Premier Peter Lougheed. They won a number of those battles, forcing Alberta to sell oil and gas to the rest of Canada for less than world prices. That saved Ontario consumers hundreds of millions of dollars, and helped Davis get re-elected. In the long-term, however, it may not have been a wise policy. Shielded from international prices, Ontarians continued to drive big cars and waste energy in their homes. Unlike its foreign competitors, Ontario industry did not adjust to the new international economic reality, did not adapt new energy-efficient technologies, and became more obsolete. Ontario industry did not even become more competitive, because wages rose to fill the vacuum created by lower energy costs. The adjustment to higher energy costs was simply put off for a few years, when it became even more painful to implement. And the bitterness injected into regional politics came back to haunt both governments when they decided that constitutional change was a desirable political goal.

Constitutional change dominated Ontario and federal politics in the early 1980s. Davis devoted his energies to it, but it is not clear what his contribution was. PM Trudeau had decided that after decades of failure, his regime would be the one to finally transfer the BNA Act from British to Canadian sovereignty. That required an agreement on how to amend the document, and that had always foundered, one reason being repeated federal incursions into provincial jurisdiction. Many provinces were opposed to the transfer of the constitution to Canadian sovereignty if that meant that the federal government could intervene in provincial responsibilities whenever it wished. The fight over the control of oil prices, when natural resources like oil were a provincial responsibility, reinforced that view, as did the federal government's recent imposition of its goals on medicare and pensions.

Davis made support for the federal position a major policy of his administration, abandoning a long tradition of Ontario leadership in the protection of provincial rights. His goal was almost certainly to reinforce Canadian unity, but the effect may have been the opposite. The constitution was transferred to Canada over the objections of Quebec, and separatism in that province was given an added boost. Premiers like Mowat, Whitney, Ferguson, Hepburn and Drew, who had worked so closely with Quebec, would not have approved. It was also unclear what Davis obtained for Ontario from his almost un-questioning support for the federal government. It is clear, though, that his support for constitutional change and patriation were widely supported in Ontario.

During this mandate Davis continued to expand rapidly health and educational facilities, especially community colleges. The growing demand for bilingual services and stronger human rights legislation was met. The first woman cabinet minister was appointed, and the ethnic vote was assiduously cultivated. With the Liberals to the right and the NDP to the left, Davis managed to occupy most of the political centre. That, and a good platform and campaign allowed him to win a majority in the election of March 19, 1981. His Conservatives gained 12 seats for 72, the Liberals held steady at 35 and the NDP lost 12 for a total of 21.

Ontario the Good seemed to be in safe hands for another five years. Davis, however, seemed to lose his touch on a number of issues. One of the more bizarre decisions he made was to buy a 25% share in an oil company. Suncor or Sunoco owned 550 service stations in Ontario, a refinery in Sarnia, and some oil fields. For some reason Davis decided to buy into it in 1981 at a cost of $650 million. The decision was taken before the issue was debated in cabinet, and the caucus knew nothing about it until it was announced. When the Treasurer, Frank Miller, heard about it, he was totally opposed, and almost resigned both over the purchase and over the fact that such a decision had been made without consulting the man responsible for the province's finances.

Three reasons were given – to give Ontario a window on the oil industry, to help increase Canadian ownership of the oil sector, and because it was a good investment and would produce large profits for the province. The first two reasons were not very convincing – Ontario did not need a "window" on the industry or to contribute to the Canadianization of the industry, especially when its 25% investment did not give it control and Suncor was not a major oil company. There had been no public demand for such a policy, and indeed, Ontarians including Conservative voters kept buying most of their gas from American companies. The only real reason seemed to be that Davis and his advisers decided it would be nice to own some oil shares, basically to play the stock market. The third reason also failed when Suncor's profits dipped sharply after the purchase.

In 1985 the Tory dynasty came to what seemed an abrupt end. Actually, it had been heading for defeat for some time in the same way that previous dynasties defeat themselves after too many years in power. The Big Blue Machine was supposed to be a near-invincible political juggernaut, but in fact it had left the Tories in a minority position from 1975 to 1981, and the Conservative popular vote had hovered around 40% or less since Davis took over. In a two-party system, the Conservatives would have long since been defeated, and the division of the opposition vote between the Liberals and the NDP is what kept it in power, not the Big Blue Machine. Luck had also run out, with the economy in decline, the North American automobile industry in serious trouble, and demand for new homes and appliances falling with the birth rate. Failure to adjust earlier to higher energy prices had left industry with obsolete equipment and uncompetitive prices once those higher costs were absorbed.

In fact, Davis' style, perhaps his shyness, his preference for taking advice from appointed party officials instead of elected MPPs, his penchant for taking major decisions without consultation and, to some, without a reason, had driven wedges between him, the cabinet, the caucus, and the party. The half of the party that was genuinely "conservative" was particularly upset with policies that were too "progressive". That had been clear as early as the 1975 election, and Davis had not done enough to move the party to the centre-right. In fact, actions like buying a share of Suncor were seen as pure socialism, the reverse of what a "progressive conservative" let alone a conservative would do.

Davis had left another ticking time-bomb in his office. Ontario governments had gradually increased funding for Catholic schools, but Grades 11, 12 and 13 were still not covered. Apparently without consulting anyone, Davis announced full funding for those grades. It seemed a safe policy as both opposition parties had demanded it. But Davis had not made it an issue, certainly an issue of justice – he simply announced it. Many Conservatives, true to their tradition, did not support it. It raised the question of why Catholics were the only religious minority to receive such support, a clear case of discrimination against the others. And it would hardly attract Catholic votes since the other parties had supported it earlier. It became a major issue in the next election, one that hurt the Conservatives far more than it helped them. It was, in short, another blunder by Davis and the Big Blue Machine.

When Davis announced his retirement in the autumn of 1984, the conservative half of the party was determined to wrest control from his left-wing, non-elected advisers. Their man was the Treasurer, Frank Miller. His conservative credentials were impeccable – born in poverty, a degree from McGill where he became bilingual, a businessman and self-made millionaire, an excellent Treasurer, representative of small-town Ontario, the cabinet minister who would never have bought Suncor. The centre-left of the party divided their votes, and Miller won the leadership in February, 1985.

Shortly after he called an election, a wise decision it seemed as the Conservatives were well ahead in the polls. But Miller was of the same generation as Davis, so this time there was no generational renewal. He sounded, dressed and acted too much like a rural businessman in a province that was overwhelmingly urban. He sounded too much like a conservative, in a province that was 2/3 centre-left. The direction his conservative supporters wanted to take the province was not the same direction as the Liberals, NDP and half the conservatives wanted to take it. The right-wing of the party had over-reacted to the mistakes of Davis, and moved too far to the right. That meant that in this election, the Liberals and NDP had more in common with each other than either did with the Tories, for the first time ever. The media sensed the change, and hounded Miller at every campaign stop.

When the votes were counted on May 2, 1985, Miller had seemingly repeated Davis' success in 1975 and 1977. The Conservatives had the most seats, at 52, and could form a minority as Davis did from 1975 to 1981. The Liberals were second with 48 seats, and had won one percentage more of the popular vote, the first time since 1937 that they had outpolled the Tories. The NDP had made a strong showing, with 25 seats. But the Liberals, the NDP and the province at large were tired of Conservative government. In fact, in passing the torch from Davis to Miller, the Tories had failed this time to renew themselves, at least, in a way the vast majority in the province wanted.

The Liberals and NDP sensed it. They made an agreement – the NDP would support a Liberal government for two years providing it followed an agenda of policies agreeable to both parties, negotiated and signed by both of them. The accord called for affirmative action, more rent control, subsidized housing and day care, better labour conditions, and a ban on extra-billing by doctors. Miller formed a new government and met the Assembly, as was his right. The Liberals and NDP defeated him on a non-confidence motion, as was their right. The lieutenant governor asked David Peterson to form a government, and he did. For only the seventh time since Confederation, Ontario had evicted a governing party.

Miller's defeat ended 42 years of Conservative rule, one of the longest dynasties in Canadian political history. It also ended the political stability Ontarians took for granted. David Peterson would go on to faithfully implement the agenda agreed with the NDP over the next two years. He then called an election, winning one of the largest landslides ever – 95 out of 130 seats, to 19 for the NDP and 16 for the Conservatives. Three years later he called a snap election, thinking that the electorate was comfortable with the new governing party.

It was a classic miscalculation, and to everyone's surprise Ontario elected its first NDP government. Bob Rae had won 74 seats to the Liberals 36 and the Tories 20. Five years later the pendulum swung wildly in the opposite direction, with a very conservative party romping to power under Mike Harris. The political gyrations reflected a roller-coaster of economic performance, with booms and busts as the economy adjusted to free trade with the United States, hi tech, economic liberalization, globalization and an accelerated pace of change. But underneath that choppy surface, Ontario continued to grow economically, to mature, to modernize, to diversify, and to maintain its status as the centre of Canada's political, economic and cultural life. That had been its role in the nineteenth and twentieth centuries, and would be so in the twenty-first.

Suggestions for Further Reading

Ontario's historiography is rather curious. Many of its historians tend to equate the province with the country, so they write Canadian history, not provincial history. This oddity was recognized decades ago by the historians themselves. They decided to fill the gap by producing biographies of the premiers. Those books contain thousands of pages of information, but the series is uneven in its coverage, and the focal point is, of course, the premiers and not the province. The histories by Bothwell, Ibbitson, Schull and White provide excellent overall accounts. Finally, almost any subject can be checked on the web, the Elections Ontario official site, for example, being the source for information on election dates and results. The following books were the main sources for the factual information summed up in our Short History of Ontario.

Bothwell, Robert, A Short History of Ontario, Edmonton, 1986
Bray, Matt and Ernie Epp, eds., A Vast and Magnificant Land: an Illustrated History of Northern Ontario, Thunder Bay, 1984
Careless, J.M.S., The Pre-Confederation Premiers, Toronto, 1980
Craig, Gerald, Upper Canada: the Formative Years, Toronto, 1980
Evans, Margaret, Sir Oliver Mowat, Toronto, 1992
Graham, Roger, Old Man Ontario: Leslie Frost, Toronto, 1990
Hoy, Clair, Bill Davis, Toronto, 1985
Humphries, Charles W., The Life and Times of James Pliny Whitney, Toronto, 1985
Ibbitson, John, Loyal No More, Toronto, 2001
Johnston, Charles M., E.C. Drury: Agrarian Idealist, Toronto, 1986
McDougall, A.K., John Robarts: His Life and Government, Toronto, 1986
Oliver, Peter, G. Ferguson: Ontario Premier, Toronto, 1977
Saywell, John T., The Life of Mitchell Hepburn, Toronto, 1991
Schull, Joseph, Ontario Since 1867, Toronto, 1978
Swainson, Donald, ed., Oliver Mowat's Ontario, Toronto, 1972
White, Randall, Ontario, 1610-1985, Toronto, 1985

Index

Dundas Street, 7
Durham, Lord, 12, 13

Eaton's, 28
Elections: (1830) 12; (1840s) 14, 16,
(1867) 20, (1871) 21, (1898) 28, (1902)
29-30, (1919) 37, (1923) 39, (1926) 41,
(1929) 43, (1934) 46, (1937) 49, (1942)
52, (1945) 54, (1949) 55, (1951, 55, and
59) 56, 59, (1963) 64-65, (1967) 65,
(1971) 68, (1975) 70, (1977) 70, (1981)
72, (1985) 73
Elgin, Lord, 14
English, England, see British
Erie natives, 2
Europe, Europeans, 1, 2, 3, 10, 28, 59
Executive Council, 5, 11, 12, 14

Family Compact, 11, 12, 13
Ferguson, G. Howard, 39-43, 44, 71
Five Nations, see Iroquois
Ford Motor Company, 28
Fort Cataraqui (see Kingston),
Fort Detroit, 3
Fort Frontenac, 3
Fort George, 9
Fort Michilimackinac, 3, 8
Fort Niagara, 3
Fort William, 3
France, French, 2, 3, 4, 34
Franco-Ontarians, French Canadians,
3, 9, 13, 15, 16, 17, 18, 24, 28, 29, 30,
32-33, 38, 41-42, 52, 53, 63, 64
French River, 1,
Frost, Leslie, 55-61, 68
Gaelic, 19, 24
Gananoque, 4
Galt, John, 10
Gamey, R.R., 29-30
General Motors, GM, 28, 48
Georgian Bay, 1, 2, 7, 21
Germans, Germany, 4, 15, 33, 34, 59
Gourlay, Robert,11
Grand River, 1, 4

Grand Trunk Railway, 14
Great Lakes, 1, 2, 3, 4, 8, 9, 11, 13, 14, 33, 55
Greeks. 59
Guelph, University, 20, 52

Hamilton, 7, 9, 22, 57
Hardy, Arthur, 28-29
Harris, John, 16
Harrison, General William Henry, 9
Hearst, Sir William, 34-36
Henry, George, 43-46
Hepburn, Mitchell, 45-55, 61, 71
Hincks, Sir Francis, 13, 14
Hindus, 64
Howe, C.D., 57
Hudson Bay, 1, 25, 33
Hudson, Henry, 2
Hudson's Bay Company, 2, 5, 17
Huron natives, 2, 3

INCO, 29
Independent Labour Party, ILP, 37
Ireland, Irish, 10, 15, 17, 21, 24
Iroquois Confederacy, natives, 2, 3, 4

James Bay, 1, 25, 45, 55
Jews, 65
Judicial Committee of the Privy Council (JCPC), 18, 24, 25, 26, 32-33
Kenora, 25
Kerr, George, 69
King, William Lyon Mackenzie, 45, 49-50, 53, 56
Kingston, 1, 3, 4, 8, 10, 21
Kitchener, 34
Labour, 35, 37-39, 46, 47
LaFontaine, Louis Hippolyte, 14
Lake Erie, 1, 4, 8, 9, 10, 15
Lake of the Woods, 4, 25, 33
Lake Huron, 1, 4, 7
Lake Nipissing, 1,
Lake Ontario, 1, 4, 7, 10, 12, 15, 57
Lake Superior, 1, 4
Lakehead University, 64

Quebec Act, 3, 4, 5
Queen's University, 15
Queenston Heights, 9
Quinte, Bay of,

Rae, Bob, 74
Raney, W.E., 38
Rebellion of 1837, 12
Reciprocity Treaty, 15, 17
Reformers, 11, 12, 13, 14, 16, 20
Regulation XVII, 33, 41-42
Responsible Government, 12, 13
Rideau Canal, River, 1, 11
Robarts, John, 60-67, 68
Robinson, Peter, 10
Roman Catholics, 3, 4, 10, 15, 16, 19, 20, 23, 24, 27, 29, 30, 33, 35, 38, 39, 47, 49, 52, 53, 64, 73
Ross, Sir George, 29
Rowell-Sirois Commission, 49-51, 53
Royal Proclamation, 3
Ryerson, Egerton, 15

Sarnia, 14, 51
Saskatchewan, 62
Sault Ste Marie, 3, 8, 19, 22, 29, 57
Scots, Scottish, Scotland, 4, 10, 15, 21, 30
Secord, Laura, 9
Sheaffe, General Rober, 9
Sikhs, 64
Simcoe, John Graves, 6, 7
Simpson's 28
Socialists, 35
Spadina Expressway, 68
St. Catharines, 64
St. Laurent, Louis, 56-61
St. Lawrence River, Seaway, 2, 3, 4, 5, 13, 14, 15, 30, 56-56
St.Michael's College, 13
Ste Marie Among the Indians, 2
Stoney Creek, battle of, 9
Strachan, Bishop John, 11
Sudbury, 22, 64
Suncor, Sunoco, 72
Sydenham, Lord Charles, 14

Talbot, Colonel Thomas, 10
Taschereau, Louis-Alexandre, 42
Tecumseh, Chief, 8, 9
Temiskaming and Northern Ontario Railway, 31
Thames, River, 1, 9
Thompson, Charles, see Sydenham
Thunder Bay, 3, 25, 56
Toronto, 7, 10, 11, 14, 15, 19, 28, 51, 56, 58, 59, 60, 63, 65
Toronto Stock Exchange, 41
Tory, Tories, see Conservatives.
Trans-Canada Highway, 45
Trans-Canada Pipeline, 56-58
Treaty of Ghent, 9
Trent River, University, 1, 64
Trinity College, 15
Trudeau, Pierre Elliott, 71

United Farmers of Ontario (UFO), 35, 36-39
United States, America, Americans, 3, 4, 5, 6, 7, 8, 9, 12, 17, 18, 21, 28, 29, 36, 57, 63, 70
University College, 15
University of Toronto, 30
Upper Canada Village, 57

Victoria College, 15

War of 1812-14, 8-9
Waterloo, 64
Welland, Welland Canal, 11
Whitney, Sir James P., 29-34, 36
Windsor, 3, 28, 57, 64
Winnipeg, 25
World War I, 29, 50, 53, 58
World War II, 49-53, 60, 61, 65

Yonge Street, 7
York (later Toronto), 7, 8, 9
Yugoslavs, 59